ISTANBUL

TRAVEL

GUIDE

Captivating Adventures Through Ottoman Splendor,

Byzantine Wonders, Turkish Landmarks, Hidden Gems, and More

Welcome Aboard, Discover
Your Limited-Time Free Bonus!

Hello, traveler! Welcome to the Captivating Travels family, and thanks for grabbing a copy of this book! Since you've chosen to join us on this journey, we'd like to offer you something special.

Check out the link below for a FREE Ultimate Travel Checklist eBook & Printable PDF to make your travel planning stress-free and enjoyable.

But that's not all - you'll also gain access to our exclusive email list with even more free e-books and insider travel tips. Well, what are you waiting for? Click the link below to join and embark on your next adventure with ease.

Access your bonus here: https://livetolearn.lpages.co/ checklist/

Or, Scan the QR code!

TABLE OF CONTENTS

INTRODUCTION

Istanbul is one of the most beautiful cities in the world. Millions of tourists worldwide visit the city every year to explore its colorful and fascinating districts and neighborhoods. It is a blend of the past and present. Istanbul's history is reflected in its ancient monuments and architecture that tell the story of a city that has survived multiple destructions and managed to stand tall until it became one of the most influential cities in the world. If you are looking for a place to explore, you will find everything you are looking for and more in Istanbul.

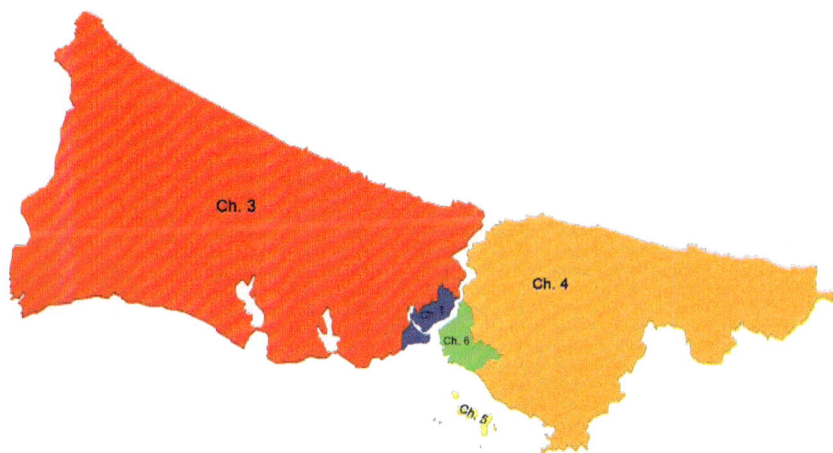

Regions in chapters.[1]

This book provides all the information you need before your journey. It is ideal for first-time travelers and easy to understand. You won't need to look for any other resources.

It starts with a detailed introduction to Istanbul. You will learn about its history, location, and association with many ancient empires. You will also learn

about Istanbulites' life, traditions, and customs. You will also learn about the city's main airports and transportation options.

The book then takes you to explore all the popular regions in Istanbul. You will begin with the city's European side and its most beautiful districts like Sultanahmet, Bakırköy, Ortaköy, Nişantaşı, Eyüp Sultan, and Sarıyer. You will then head to the Eastern side, called the "Asian side," and discover its magnificent districts like Beykoz, Pendik, Sancaktepe, Maltepe, and Ataşehir.

You will then take a tour of the breathtaking Prince Islands and explore its peaceful and interesting districts like Büyükada, Heybeliada, Burgazada, and Kınalıada.

Next, add the tourist hotspots in the Asian and European sections and all the famous landmarks and locations in Kadıköy, Üsküdar, Beyoğlu, Beşiktaş, Fatih, and Şişli.

Each district mentioned includes its historical background, fun facts, main attractions, transportation, fun experiences, family activities, restaurants, popular stores, an en-

tertainment section, sports and leisure, and accommodations.

You don't have to waste time preparing itineraries for your journey. You will find multiple thematic or traveler-oriented programs in every district to enjoy your vacation and explore everything the city offers in the suggested itineraries towards the end of the book.

It isn't just Istanbul worth visiting. There are exciting destinations just a couple of hours away from the city that you shouldn't miss. You will discover places like Edirne, Bursa, Princes' Islands, Sapanca and Maşukiye, and İznik.

One of the main challenges tourists face when visiting a new country is the language barrier. You will find many Turkish phrases and their meaning to communicate easily with the locals and make new friends.

Now, head to the first chapter and start your journey.

CHAPTER 1

GET TO KNOW ISTANBUL

If you Google the most popular tourist destinations worldwide, you will find Istanbul on every list. About 17 million people visit the city annually, many of whom return as they can't get enough of Turkey's gem. With its long history, famous landmarks, rich culture, tasty cuisine, and popular nightlife, Istanbul has everything to satisfy your wanderlust.

Istanbul map.[2]

Istanbul is a mix of the old and new. You will be transported back in time as you explore its ancient monuments. The city that has witnessed the rise and fall of many empires will speak to you and tell you its incredible story. You will also be amazed by its culture and modern lifestyle. Istanbul is a blend of the

East and the West, a timeless city that is impossible to define or sum up in a few words.

This chapter takes you on a journey in this enchanting city to see why it's on many people's bucket lists.

ISTANBUL'S STRATEGIC GEOGRAPHICAL LOCATION

Istanbul's strategic geographical location is one of the many characteristics that make it Turkey's most famous city. It is one of the few cities in the world that is a part of Asia and Europe. The eastern part is in Asia, and the western is in Europe, and it acts as a bridge between the two continents. Istanbul is divided by the famous Bosporus Strait, which is 19 miles (30 kilometers) long and connects the north's Black Sea to the south's Sea of Marmara. It is also a seaport, the closest European city to Asia and the closest Asian city to Europe.

When the Romans ruled, they built the city on seven hills to mimic other Roman cities. Just like in Rome, the city walls surrounded the hills.

Thanks to Istanbul's strategic location, the city was the region's main trade route linking the Mediterranean Basin, the Balkans, the Russian steppe, the Caucasus, the Horn of Africa, the Arabian Peninsula, Iran, and Europe. Venice was also a central trading route at the time. Although the two cities traded, they were mainly rivals and enemies.

Trading ships sailed from the Black Sea to the Mediterranean Sea. Horse and camel caravans often took routes stretching from Europe to the Anatolian Plateau, heading east, south, and north.

Istanbul's location made it the envy of Europe and the Middle East. Many countries' leaders recognized its unique position. They wanted to control the city, leading to wars and crusades that have impacted Istanbul to this day.

ISTANBUL'S DISTINCTIVE DISTRICTS AND NEIGHBORHOODS

Istanbul is Turkey's largest city, with 39 districts. Until recently, there were only 32 districts. However, its growing population led to urban restructuring, and additional districts were created.

ISTANBUL'S HISTORY

Istanbul is one of the world's most ancient cities and has a long and rich history. It was a part of many empires that rose and fell. Interestingly, the city wasn't always called Istanbul and has undergone multiple name changes throughout its history.

BYZANTIUM

Early settlers inhabited Istanbul in 2 BC and lived in the Asian section. However, it wasn't a city back then. In 7 BCE, Greek King Byzas and his colonists arrived in the Bosporus region. They were fascinated by its location and decided to establish a colony and settle there. Byzas knew that this region would prosper one day because his oracle Delphi told him to go to the land of the blind. This unusual description of ancient Istanbul was due to Byzas believing that early settlers were too blind to overlook a region with such a strategic and magnificent location. Byzas was so fond of it that he named it after himself, Byzantium.

In the 5th century, Persians invaded Byzantium and destroyed it. In 479 B.C., Spartan general Pausanias reconstructed it and returned it to its former glory. In 409 B.C., the Athenians occupied the land for four years until the Spartans invaded it again. However, in 390 B.C., Athenians regained control of Byzantium.

Byzantium was also a part of the Macedonian empire and was under the rule of Alexander the Great for years. In 191 B.C. the city gained its independence, but this didn't last

long. In 197, Roman Emperor Septimius Severus and his army attacked Byzantium and destroyed it. However, he later rebuilt the city in the image of Eastern Roman colonies. It stayed a part of the Roman Empire for over a thousand years and underwent many changes, including its name.

CONSTANTINOPLE

In 324 B.C., Roman Emperor Constantine the Great rebuilt Byzantium as a part of the Roman Empire. He added many Roman monuments to the city and made sure it stood out as he planned to honor it with a new name in 330 B.C. He named the city Constantinople after himself and made it the capital of the Roman Empire. During this time, it prospered and became one of the region's most influential and powerful cities.

In 395, Roman Emperor Theodosius the Great passed away. His two sons divided the Empire into Eastern and Western parts, and it was never reunited again. Constantinople was no longer the capital of the Roman Empire.

In the 400s, it became the capital of the Eastern Roman Empire, also called the Byzantine Empire, which became a Greek colony. Gradually, Constantinople started to lose its

Roman identity and was hugely influenced by the Greeks.

Because of Constantinople's strategic position, it became the center of diplomacy, culture, and commerce. In 532, the people weren't pleased with how Roman Emperor Justinian I handled certain political issues, leading to one of the most devastating events in Constantinople's history, the Nika Riot. This resulted in an unprecedented loss of human life and the destruction of the city.

The city was rebuilt again including many of its monuments like the Hagia Sophia church, which later became a mosque. At the time, the city became the Greek Orthodox Church's center.

For decades, Constantinople prospered under the reign of the Byzantine Empire for many reasons, including its unique location. However, its success was a blessing and a curse as it drew the eyes of the world to it and attracted many invaders. For centuries, many Middle Eastern countries attacked the city. In 1204, it was defiled by the Crusaders and remained under their control for years. Eventually, it became the center of the Catholic Latin Empire.

Constant rivalry existed between the Greek Orthodox Church and the Catholic Latin Empire. Con-

stantinople's association with them meant it was dragged into the middle of this, resulting in devastating consequences. The city became defenseless, its population declined, and it went bankrupt. In 1261, while the city was still reeling, it was recaptured by the Nicaea Empire and joined the Byzantine Empire again.

During this time, the Ottoman Turks were gaining power and invading Constantinople's neighboring cities, cutting it off from the rest of the world.

ISTANBUL

After the previous events, Constantinople became vulnerable and an easy target for invaders. In 1453, Ottoman Sultan Mehmed II and his troops conquered the city and declared it the Ottoman Empire's capital. They changed its name to Istanbul. Sultan Mehmed II wanted to erase all remains of Greek and Roman influence and turn it into an Ottoman city.

He rejuvenated Istanbul and brought back all Greek Orthodox and Catholics who fled the city. He built the Grand Bazaar, which is still standing to this day. He also created a diverse community of Jewish, Christian, and Muslim families in the city. The sultan also built large mosques like the Fa-

tih Mosque and public baths, hospitals, and schools.

Suleiman the Magnificent ruled the Ottoman Empire from 1520 to 1566. During that time, the city witnessed an architectural and artistic revolution, making Istanbul a major commercial, political, and cultural center. Its population had also grown to 1 million residents. It remained under the Ottoman Empire's rule until the First World War.

In 1923, the Turkish people gained their independence, and the Republic of Turkey was established. Istanbul became a part of the country but wasn't its capital. Ankara is the capital of Turkey. In the early years, investors turned their attention to the new and exciting city of Ankara and ignored Istanbul.

In the 1940s and 1950s, Istanbul returned to its previous glory, constructing avenues, boulevards, and public squares. In the 1970s, the city's population increased rapidly, and became a major city.

Now, Istanbul is the home to many historical monuments that were added to the UNESCO World Heritage list. In 2010, it was chosen as the European capital of culture.

ISTANBUL AS A HISTORICAL AND CULTURAL HUB

Istanbul was the capital of many empires, and each has left its mark on the city, making it a historical and cultural hub. Walking down the streets of Istanbul, you will find many cultural centers, including bookstores, libraries, and theaters.

One of Istanbul's most famous cultural centers is The Foundation, which organizes events like movies, jazz, theater, music, and festivals. Another is the Ataturk Cultural Center, which acts as an opera house and has libraries, a cinema hall, and a theater. Hodjapasha Cultural Center is another testament to the city's cultural influence. It is near the city's most famous monument, the Hagia Sophia. It was initially a public bath. Although the building is a historic landmark, it is decorated with modern lights and colors, making it one of the most marvelous places in the city. It is famous for its Rumi dance shows and other traditional dance displays.

ISTANBUL'S UNIQUE POSITION

Istanbul is Turkey's most popular city, and it stands out from all other cities in the country, Europe, and the Middle East. It is one of the few cities in the region where you can take a 15-minute ferry from one continent to another. Istanbul also has many architectural buildings and monuments from the Roman Empire, the Byzantine Empire, the Latin Empire, and the Ottoman Empire. You will find traces of its rich and diverse history wherever you go.

Istanbul also has breathtaking natural scenery like the Prince Islands and the Bosphorus Strait. It is also Europe's most populous city.

Istanbul's European side is one of the most extensive parts of the city and has 25 districts. It is divided by a natural stream called "The Golden Horn" that drains into the Bosporus Strait.

The European section is popular among tourists since it's home to some of the most famous historical monuments in the world, like Kapalıçarşı pronounced "kah-PAH-luh CHAR-shuh" meaning "Covered market," the Topkapi Palace Museum, Sultan Suleymaniye Mosque, the Blue Mosque, and Hagia Sophia.

Istanbul's Asian section has 14 districts and multiple attractions like Kadıköy market, Bağdat Caddesi Avenue, Caddebostan Dalyan Park, Haydarpaşa Train Station, Beylerbeyi Palace, and Çamlıca mosque.

LIFE IN ISTANBUL

Have you ever wondered what characterizes Istanbulites? You can only understand a city by learning about its people, their traditions, and lifestyle.

ISTANBULITES ARE HOSPITABLE

Istanbulites, and all Turkish people, are famous for their hospitality. You can meet a local, and after an hour, they will invite you to dinner at their home and introduce you to their family. They are very generous people and treat their guests with respect.

ISTANBULITES ARE PUNCTUAL PEOPLE

If you have an appointment with an Istanbulite, expect them to be on time. However, if they are ever late, understand it isn't their fault. Istanbul is a large city, and traffic can sometimes be a problem. However, they will do their best not to keep you waiting.

NO SHOES AT HOME

In most Istanbulites' homes, you must remove your shoes before entering. They always keep slippers at the door so guests can wear them in the house to prevent dirt and dust from getting inside. They will also offer you cologne, or as they call it, "Kolonya," to disinfect your hands.

ISTANBULITES LOVE TEA

Tea is a popular beverage in Turkey.[3]

Tea is one of the most popular beverages in Turkey. They usually drink a cup at breakfast and multiple other times during the day. Even though Istanbul has Starbucks and other cafes, nothing is as popular as their traditional tea.

ISTANBULITES VALUE LOYALTY

They love their family and friends and are highly loyal to them. If you have a Turkish friend, expect that they will always be by your side and have your back.

ISTANBULITES ARE DIRECT

Istanbul is fast-paced; people are always in a hurry, and many don't have time for pleasantries. Istanbulites are direct and say things as they are. They prefer to use a few words to express themselves or just nod or shake their head in response.

ISTANBULITES LOVE LOVE

Have you ever watched a Turkish TV show or dizi? Most of the stories are about love. Istanbulites are romantic and still believe that true love can conquer all. When they fall in love, they fall hard and deep.

ISTANBULITES LIKE GETTING PERSONAL

If you have a conversation with someone from Istanbul, they may ask personal questions like "Are you single?" or "Do you have children?" They aren't trying to cross boundaries; they just don't mind discussing personal details, even with strangers.

ISTANBUL TRADITIONS

+ Although they don't celebrate Christmas, you will find Christmas decorations around the city during this time of the year.

+ Circumcision ceremonies are very popular in the city.

+ They believe that someone's envy could harm them, so they use blue glass eyes to ward off negative energy.

+ They greet each other with a kiss on the cheek, and they greet elderly people by kissing their hands.

+ Brides often serve their grooms a cup of coffee with a pinch of salt in it to test their love. If he drinks it without complaining, he truly loves her.

+ Fortune tellers are very popular in the city, and many, especially girls, seek their advice when they fall in love.

ISTANBULITES LIFESTYLE

+ They enjoy going to the opera, ballet, and concerts

+ Istanbul is famous for its nightlife, and you will find nightclubs and bars all over the city

+ Family and friends enjoy getting together and eating out in any of Istanbul's restaurants

+ Many of the most popular clothing brands are sold in Istanbul

ISTANBUL COSMOPOLITAN FABRIC

Istanbul is a pretty diverse city. Its history shows how it welcomed different empires and cultures and managed to adapt to all the transformations throughout the years. The city prides itself on being a cosmopolitan metropolis. It doesn't fall under one category. It is a pro-western, democratic, Muslim, and secular city. No matter what your beliefs are or how you identify yourself, you will feel at home in Istanbul.

The city still holds on to its Islamic identity. It is home to 3000 thousand mosques which are all considered architectural masterpieces. However, it still cherishes its Christian roots, as you will see from the many eye-catching churches around the city.

Many different ethnic groups live in Istanbul like the Uyghurs, Crimean Tatars, Uzbeks, Karakalpaks, Karachays, Tatars, Azeris, and Turks. There are also Indo-Europeans like Greeks, Gorani, Hamshenis, Armenians, Pomaks, Albanians, Bosniaks, Zaza-Dimli Kurds, and Kurds. You also have Semitic-speaking people like Jews, Arabs, and Assyrians. One can't forget the Caucasian-speaking people like Chechens, Laz, Georgians, and Circassians.

It is rare to find a city with historical, religious, and cultural diversity like that of Istanbul.

AN IN-DEPTH LOOK INTO ISTANBUL'S LOCAL CULTURE

One of the most popular aspects of Istanbul is its local culture. Travelers are often left in awe of the city's cuisine, art scene, and customs.

ISTANBUL'S CELEBRATED CUISINE

Istanbul is famous for its tasty dishes. You haven't truly lived until you try Istanbul's cuisine.

TURKISH MEATBALLS (KÖFTE)

Köfte is one of the most popular dishes in Istanbul and you can find it anywhere in the city's streets. It is usually made with beef, parsley, and onions. You can eat it in a sandwich in the streets or with yogurt and a side dish at any local restaurant like Tarihi Sultanahmet Köftecisi Selim Usta.

TURKISH PIZZA (LAHMACUN)

Lahmacun is also known as Turkish Pizza.[4]

Lahmacun is made with round dough, topped with vegetables, sauce, minced meat, and Turkish spices and herbs. Some restaurants also add lemon juice on top. If you don't like these toppings, no problem. Most restaurants offer a wide variety of ingredients. One of the best places that serve Lahmacun is Borsam Taşfırın in the Kadıköy fish market area.

BAKED POTATO (KUMPIR)

This popular street food should be the first thing you try when you arrive in Istanbul. The potatoes are baked in the oven, then they add cheese and local butter for a mouth-watering flavor. You can also change the topping and customize it to your liking. You can add tomatoes, olives, mushrooms, red cabbage, and more. You will find many places in Ortaköy that serve Kumpir.

BAKLAVA

You can't have a meal without dessert, and Baklava will satisfy your sugar craving. It is a crispy delight made with dough, filled with hazelnuts, walnuts, or pistachios, and topped with syrup or honey. You will find this mouthwatering dessert in most restaurants in the city. However, you should only eat it from an experienced chef to savor the unique experience. Karaköy Güllüoğlu is one of Istanbul's most famous Baklava restaurants.

TURKISH BREAKFAST

Turkish breakfast isn't just a meal but an experience. It is delicious and filling. There will be boiled eggs, cucumbers, lettuce, cold-cut meats, cheese, olives, butter, and fresh bread. You can have Turkish breakfast in your hotel or any restaurant in the city.

TURKISH COFFEE

Istanbulites love their coffee, and none is as tasty as their Turkish coffee. It is one of the oldest beverages in the country, dating back to the Ottoman Empire. It is also a part of many rituals like when a man and his family go to his betrothed home and ask for her hand in marriage. Coffee is usually served with a delicious Turkish delight called *lokum*. You can have Turkish coffee anywhere in the city, but it is best to try it in local and authentic places like Bebek Kahve.

ISTANBUL'S VIBRANT ART SCENE

Istanbul's unique position between the West and the East greatly impacted its art scene. Each civilization that once called Istanbul home left its mark on the city, and created a rich and diverse artistic heritage. The city has everything from ancient architecture to majestic palaces and modern art.

Istanbul has one of the most vibrant contemporary art scenes in the world. You will find a blend of funky installation pieces, photography, international avant-garde, and high-end art.

If you love art, check out Istanbul Modern, where you will find 20th and 21st-century Turkish paintings. You should also check Boğazkesen

Caddesi Street. There are many famous galleries there that sell paintings by famous Turkish artists, some sell for $30,000.

ISTANBUL TRADITIONAL CRAFTS

Istanbulites create one-of-a-kind crafts, thanks again to their strategic location and particular history. Craftsmen mix their rich past with modern traditions while adding their imagination and creativity to create distinctive pieces.

You will find craft shops on many of Istanbul's streets. The locals will happily teach you how to create handicrafts and don't shy away from sharing their secrets. All you have to do is ask. You will find all types of Turkish crafts like embroidery, ceramics, earthenware, jewelry, quilts, and more.

ISTANBUL CUSTOMS

Understanding a city's customs before visiting is necessary to avoid any misunderstandings. Locals will also be pleased that you took the time to learn about their culture, customs, and traditions.

+ *Men greet each other with a firm handshake and make eye contact*

+ *Friends and families greet each other by hugging or patting one another on the back*

+ *Close women friends hug and kiss each other on the cheek*

+ *Other women greet each other by gently shaking hands*

+ *Men who meet Turkish women for the first time should follow their lead. If she extends her hand, shake it. If she offers her cheek, kiss it. If she doesn't extend her hands, just nod and say "Merhaba," meaning "Hello." Religious women don't shake hands with men.*

+ *When a Turkish person raises their eyebrows or tilts their head backward, it means "No"*

+ *Placing a hand on the chest or heart expresses gratitude or greeting*

SPORTS AND LEISURE ACTIVITIES IN ISTANBUL

Many Istanbulites, especially young ones, enjoy watching and playing sports. Soccer is the most popular sport in the city. There are five soccer teams from Istanbul playing in the Turkish Premier League: Buyuksehir Belediye, Kasımpaşa S.K., Beşiktaş J.K., Galatasaray S.K., Fenerbahçe SK (Fenerbahçe). The most popular soccer stadiums in the city

are Vodafone Stadium, Ali Sami Yen Spor Kompleksi, Şükrü Saracoğlu Stadium, and Atatürk Olympic Stadium. Istanbulites also enjoy watching basketball, motorsports, horse races, and tennis.

Istanbulites have other interests as well. They enjoy spending their free time at çay bahçesi or tea gardens. They are usually casual places with affordable prices. You get to have a cup of tea in a quiet spot with gorgeous scenery. Some of the most popular tea gardens in the city are Bebek Kahve, Çengelköy Çınaraltı, Dolmabahçe Çay Bahçesi, and Moda Çay Bahçesi.

The city is also famous for its bustling bazaars. These markets are in every part of the city. Spices, books, accessories, clothes, etc., whatever you are looking for, you will surely find at a Turkish bazaar. Some of the must-see bazaars are Sahaflar Çarşısı (Book Bazaar), Fatih Çarşamba (Wednesday) Market, Egyptian Spice Bazaar, İstiklal Caddesi (Istiklal Street), Arasta Bazaar, and Grand Bazaar.

ISTANBUL'S MOST FAMOUS PERSONALITIES

Many famous people who were born in Istanbul managed to achieve so much to make any Istanbulite proud. Although some historical figures might have made questionable decisions, they still influenced the city's identity.

MURAD IV

Date of Birth: 7/27/1612.

Place of Birth: Topkapi Palace, Constantinople, Ottoman Empire.

Occupation: Sultan of the Ottoman Empire from 1623 to 1640.

Known For: His brutal methods and for restoring the state's authority.

Murad was only 11 when he became a sultan. He played a huge role in the Ottoman–Safavid War, which ended with the Ottoman victory. He died in 1640 at the age of 27.

HONORIUS

Date of Birth: 9/9/384.

Place of Birth: Constantinople.

Occupation: Roman emperor from 393 to 423.

Known For: His chaotic reign and witnessing the sacking of Rome for the first time in 800 years.

He became a ruler with his brother at the age of seven. After his father, Theodosius I's death, he and his brother Arcadius divided the Roman Empire. Honorius was the Emperor of the Western part at the age of ten.

ARDA TURAN

Date of Birth: 30/1/1987.

Place of Birth: Fatih, Istanbul.

Occupation: Soccer player at Galatasaray S.K.

Known For: His dribbling skills, ball control, and scoring 17 goals for Turkey's national team.

Turan is the fifth-most capped Turkish soccer player. He is also a humanitarian, a goodwill ambassador who spends his time helping sick children.

IREM KARAMETE

Date of Birth: 6/20/1993.

Place of Birth: Istanbul.

Occupation: Turkish fencer.

Known For: Being the first Turkish to compete in the Summer Olympics since 1984.

Irem began her career at the age of ten and won ten Turkish championships from 2011 to 2019.

NESLIHAN ATAGÜL DOĞULU

Date of Birth: 8/20/1992.

Place of Birth: Istanbul.

Occupation: Turkish actress.

Known For: Kara Sevda or Endless Love, one of the most successful Turkish TV shows of all time, which won an international Emmy award in 2017.

Neslihan is a successful and talented Turkish actress recognized in Turkey, Europe, Asia, and the Middle East.

NAVIGATING ISTANBUL

Although Istanbul is famous for its traffic, getting around the city is easier than you think. Most major attractions and historic landmarks are relatively close to each other, so you can either walk or use one of the city's multiple transport options.

TRAMS

Istanbul has four modern tram lines. The most popular one is the T1, which starts from the Kabataş ferry terminal, runs across the Galata Bridge, and takes you to the Sultanahmet neighborhood. Another tram is the T5, located near the Golden Horn and stops in various neighborhoods like Eyüp, Balat, and Fener. The T3 tram passes through the Kadıköy district on the Asian side.

FERRIES

Riding an Istanbul ferry is a once-in-a-lifetime experience. You can ride one and cross the Bosphorus between Beşiktaş, Kabataş, Karaköy, and Eminönü on the European section and Üsküdar and Kadıköy on the Asian side. You will also find ferries to take you to the Princes' Islands and the Golden Horn.

METROS

Metros are the fastest method of transportation in Istanbul. Metro lines connect to every part of the city. Tourists usually use the M2 lines between Hacıosman and Yenikapı, which take you to popular shopping districts like Şişhane in Beyoğlu, Taksim Square, and Levent. The Marmaray metro can take you to the Asian section through an underground tunnel.

USEFUL WEBSITES AND RESOURCES

Check these websites for planning, accommodations, and activities in Istanbul.

WEBSITES FOR TRAVEL PLANNING

- ✓ https://istanbul.com/
- ✓ dhmi.gov.tr/Sayfalar/AnaSayfa.aspx
- ✓ https://www.metro.istanbul/
- ✓ https://ido.com.tr/tr/
- ✓ https://wanderlog.com/tp/9622/istanbul-trip-planner
- ✓ https://turkeytravelplanner.com/go/Istanbul/index.html
- ✓ https://triptile.com/istanbul
- ✓ https://istanbul-tourist-information.com/en/plan-your-trip-to-istanbul/

WEBSITES FOR ACCOMMODATIONS

- ✓ *https://booking.com/city/tr/istanbul.en-gb.html*
- ✓ *https://agoda.com/city/istanbul-tr. html?cid=1844104&ds=IXjlbMSFjQ6VaoGu*
- ✓ *https://www.lastminute.com/hotels/tr_turkey/istanbul-d1511153601*
- ✓ *https://hotels.com/de1341107/hotels-istanbul-turkey/?locale=en_GB&pos=HCOM_ME&siteid=310000033*
- ✓ *https://www.otelz.com/en*

WEBSITES FOR ACTIVITIES

- ✓ *https://www.visitturkey.in/*
- ✓ *https://lonelyplanet.com/turkey/istanbul*
- ✓ *https://goturkiye.com/*
- ✓ *https://istanbul.ktb.gov.tr/#*
- ✓ *https://timeout.com/istanbul*
- ✓ *https://tripadvisor.com/Attractions-g293974-Activities-Istanbul.html*
- ✓ *https://viator.com/Istanbul/d585*
- ✓ *https://www.headout.com/things-to-do-city-istanbul/*
- ✓ *www.headout.com/things-to-do-city-istanbul/*

N.B. All the prices, working hours, and addresses mentioned here were correct at the time of writing this book. Please double-check this information online before your trip.

Whatever experience travelers are looking for, they will find it in Istanbul. The city that combines the East and West cultures while maintaining its own unique identity is one of the most fascinating places you will ever visit. With its hospitable people, delicious cuisine, magnificent architecture, beautiful scenery, large bazaars, and exciting nightlife, there isn't a dull moment in Istanbul.

2

TO AND FROM THE AIRPORT

Now that you have learned everything about Istanbul, you are eager to start planning your trip. One of the most common questions first-time travelers often ask is, "What should I do after I land in my destination?"

This chapter answers all your questions and provides you with information about Istanbul's main airports, available transportation, and tips on navigating the airport.

ISTANBUL AIRPORT (IST)

Istanbul Airport.[5]

Although Istanbul Airport is relatively new, it is the city's main airport. It is one of the Turkish government's biggest achievements and can host 200 million passengers. It is located on the European side in the Çatalca- Göktürk-Ar-

navutköy, about 32 miles from Kadıköy and 25 miles from Taksim. The airport stands between Akpinar village and Tayakadin. It serves destinations in 110 countries and over 350 domestic trips. It also has the largest duty-free area in the world. At the time of writing, the airport has four runways and one functioning terminal, which is the biggest terminal worldwide. It is divided into two areas: Arrivals and Departures. The government is planning to add three other terminal buildings.

The IST provides unmatched facilities and services with cutting-edge technology. It is also environmentally friendly. However, the airport has two disadvantages. It has only two security control areas, one for international flights and the other for domestic flights. As a result, airport procedures can take a long time. The other disadvantage is the long distance between the terminal central areas and the boarding areas.

TRANSPORTATION

+ Istanbul Metro Line M11

+ Havaist bus

+ Car rental

+ Istanbul airport transfer

+ Airport taxi

SERVICES AND AMENITIES

✓ Special services for people with disabilities

✓ Information kiosks

✓ Tour operators and travel agencies

✓ Wi-Fi

✓ Pet rooms

✓ Airport Hotel

✓ Lounges

✓ Spa

✓ Business Center

✓ Art galleries

✓ Prayer rooms

✓ Lost and found offices

✓ Family services

✓ ATMs

✓ Currency exchange areas

✓ Banks

✓ Pharmacies

✓ Medical services

✓ Baggage wrapping

✓ Restaurants

✓ Bars

✓ Retail stores

✓ Duty-free area

SABIHA GÖKÇEN INTERNATIONAL AIRPORT (SAW)

Sabiha Gökçen International Airport (SAW) is in the Asian section 20 miles southeast of the city center of Taksim and 15 miles from Kadıköy. It was named after Sabiha Gökçen, the adoptive daughter of the founding father of the Republic of Turkey, Mustafa Kemal Atatürk. Sabiha was an international hero as she was the first female combat pilot in the world to join the army.

SAW has two terminals for international and domestic flights. It also acts as a hub for Pegasus Airlines and Anadolu Jet. It is the second-busiest airport in Turkey. It serves about 36 million passengers. You can access this airport by public transportation, roads, or major highways.

SERVICES AND AMENITIES

- ✓ Transit hotel
- ✓ Lounges
- ✓ Restaurants
- ✓ Duty-free shops
- ✓ Banks
- ✓ ATMs
- ✓ Baggage services
- ✓ Fast track zones
- ✓ Lost and found
- ✓ Prayer rooms

TRANSPORTATION OPTIONS IN ISTANBUL

You don't need to carry money to use public transportation. You just need an electronic card called an Istanbulkart. You can use it in any transport system, and it can last for your whole stay in the city. You can buy it upon arrival from Istanbul Airport, Sabiha Gökçen International Airport, major boat or bus terminals, vending machines, service stations, and kiosks (booths). You can also purchase Istanbul Welcome Cards Premium for tourists. They offer great deals, and you can use them for cruises and tours on the Bosphorus.

These are some of the best transport options from the airports to the city center.

ISTANBUL AIRPORT (IST) TRANSPORTATION

- ✓ **Taxis**: They are available 24/7 at Istanbul Airport. It takes about 40 minutes to get to Taksim Squarey6t and costs about $55.
- ✓ **Private Airport Transfer (VIP Transfer):** Book a private ride if you want to spoil yourself. It is more comfortable and convenient.

These rides are more expensive, but depending on the car and the services, you will find different prices. You can easily book a ride online, and it will take you to the city center in 36 minutes under normal traffic conditions.

✓ **Metros**: They are available 24/7, convenient, and cheap. They will take you to your destination in 50 minutes, and the ticket costs less than $1. The M11 Gayrettepe metro connects the airport to the city. However, it isn't finished, and you will need to transfer to Line M2 to reach Taksim.

✓ **Bus**: It costs about $4 and will take you to Taksim in 90 minutes. Buses are available around the clock and depart every 20 minutes.

✓ **Shuttle Bus**: This method is very popular and costs about $4. It will take you 36 minutes to reach Taksim under normal traffic conditions. These buses are always available at the airport.

✓ **Sabiha Gokcen Airport (SAW) Transportation**

✓ **Taxi**: A ride from SAW to Kadıköy costs about $ 30-40 and takes 40 minutes to 1 hour, depending on traffic.

Taxis are always available at the airport.

✓ **Private Airport Transfer**: This is the most comfortable option, especially if you have children. The car will take you directly to a hotel in 40 minutes to 1 hour, depending on traffic. You can easily book a ride online.

✓ **Metro**: You can take the M4 line to reach Kadıköy. The trip takes about 40 minutes and costs less than $1.

✓ **Buses**: Buses are very cheap, costing only $1; the E11 bus line takes you directly to Kadıköy in 70 minutes. Buses are available 24/7.

✓ **Shuttle bus**: A bus departs every 30 minutes to Kadıköy, Taksim, and Yenisahra. It takes 60 to 90 minutes to get to Kadıköy and costs about $5. Shuttle buses are always available at the airport.

TIPS ON NAVIGATING ISTANBUL AIRPORT

✦ Passengers should check in at entrance doors number 3 and 4.

✦ Complete procedures at aisles F, G, H, and J.

- Aisles A to C and M to S are for non-Turkish Airlines Flights.

- Aisle L is for Star Alliance Gold card holders and business class passengers.

- Aisle K is for flights from Canada, the U.K., and the U.S.

- Aisle H is for unaccompanied minors and families.

- Aisle G is for large groups and passengers with disabilities.

- Asile E is for self-check-ins.

LUGGAGE STORAGE OPTIONS

There are two luggage storage options at IST.

LEFT LUGGAGE OFFICES

This is an easy and safe option to store your belongings for a long period. You will find these offices at the airport's main building on the arrival floor opposite gate 13 and close to the domestic gate. They are available 24/7. To use this service, you must fill out an application and present your passport and boarding pass.

STORAGE LOCKERS

This option is for passengers looking to store their luggage for a short period. These lockers are located on the departure levels near Gates 1 and 6. You can rent small, medium, or large lockers, and rental offices are available 24/7. You will get access to your locker after paying a fee via credit card or cash.

CURRENCY EXCHANGE

You can convert your money into Turkish lira at any of the many currency exchange counters in the airport.

TOURIST INFORMATION CENTER

If you have any questions, head to the tourist information center on the international Arrivals floor. They are available every day from 9 AM to 7 pm. You can also email them at turizmisleri34@ktb.gov.tr.

TIPS ON NAVIGATING SABIHA GÖKÇEN INTERNATIONAL AIRPORT

- Counters A to H are for departure check-ins.

- International remote gates are 301A/B-306A/B.

- Boarding gate areas are 203A/B – 206/AB, 201 - 202A/B, and 207 - 208AB.

LUGGAGE STORAGE OPTIONS

You can leave your luggage at the Baggage Storage Office located on the international arrival level for a daily fee, depending on your luggage size. They are available 24/7, and you can contact them at this number: +90 216 588 88 02.

CURRENCY EXCHANGE

Offices are available 24/7 to exchange your currency for Turkish lira. They are located in the International Arrivals Baggage Claim Area, Arrivals Hall of the Terminal Building, Air Side, and International Departures Hall Land Side.

You can contact them on this number: +90 588 52 10.

TOURIST INFORMATION CENTER

The airport has four information desks- the Domestic Hall, the International Hall, and the Departures Level.

TURKISH CUSTOM REGULATIONS

+ *You will need an entry visa to enter Turkey. It costs $20 and is valid for three months.*

+ *Besides personal items, you can bring one laptop, a pair of binoculars, personal spotting equipment, a camera, necessary medical items, and gifts that cost $300 or less.*

+ *Weapons, sharp objects, and camping and diving knives aren't allowed without a permit.*

+ *Marijuana and other narcotics are prohibited.*

+ *When departing, you should have a receipt for everything you bought*

Study this information before leaving and refer to it after arrival to guarantee a smooth trip without any issues.

3

THE EUROPEAN SIDE

Divided by the magnificent Bosphorus Bridge, Istanbul has two sides, the European and the Asian. To begin exploring the many districts of Istanbul, this chapter will introduce you to the European side of the city. It showcases the history and background of its stunning districts, along with some recommendations for memorable experiences and activities.

HISTORICAL AND BACKGROUND INFORMATION

As you step into the Western side of the Bosphorus Strait of Turkey, the natural boundary between the two continents, you are greeted with an unmistakably European flare with distinct Mediterranean undertones. Housing the city's most stunning and historically prominent landmarks, the European side of Istanbul encompasses two-thirds of the Turkish capital's population. Beyond being highly popular among tourists, the European side of Istanbul is also the city's most populated area, and for an excellent reason. It features Istanbul's most famous commercial areas, vibrant neighborhoods, and everything else that shapes this area into a major economic hub in Turkey.

The European side of Istanbul.[6]

Home to some of the city's most gorgeous and historical landmarks, you'll find the European side of Istanbul. It's where you'll get old meets new and modern meets traditional. The traditional neighborhoods of Istanbul are located on the peninsula, while the modern ones are north of the Golden Horn.

While dividing the two continents, the Bosphorus Strait connection also acts as a bridge between the two parts of the city. The two parts are strongly linked through the waterway course, which enables shipping and transportation in modern times. It also acted as a strong line of defense in ancient times.

Lying south of the European side of Istanbul, the Marmara Sea is connected to the Mediterranean Sea through the Bosphorus, explaining European Istanbul's strong connection to the Mediterranean. At the same time, the Marmara Sea also plays a crucial role in the historical, transportation, and cultural aspects of the city's Western side.

From the European side of Istanbul, ports and coastal areas provide access to the city's many landmarks and cultural and economic hubs. For example, the neighborhoods of Eminonu and Karakoy offer a wide range of maritime activ-

ity through their bustling terminals. Serving as gateways for domestic and international ferry services, these terminals connect the European side of Istanbul with various destinations beyond the city.

Moderating Istanbul's temperature and providing much-needed refreshment through light breezes during the scorching summer months, the Marmara Sea positively influences the climate of Istanbul's European side, which is another reason behind its popularity among tourists. The stunning deep blue waters, many watersport opportunities, and picturesque islands further add to the city's scenic charm and allure.

Forming a natural harbor on the city's European side, the Golden Horn Bosphorus inlet resembles a horn (hence the name) and is famous for the Galata Bridge. Historically, several major neighborhoods of Istanbul have evolved around this harbor, shaping it into one of the city's most vibrant areas.

The densely populated areas are punctuated by lush green spaces, giving way to an interesting and enjoyable landscape. This is further enriched by the picturesque waterfront, which divides the busy winding streets of the European side from the quiet, residential experience on the Asian side.

Did You Know?

The European side of Istanbul is further divided into two major regions: the old town (also known as the Historic Peninsula), centering on historical tourism, and the new part, developed as a modern addition to the city on the West side of the Bosphorus.

THE OLD PART OF EUROPEAN ISTANBUL

The traditional part of Istanbul showcases the city's global side. Located on the Historic Peninsula, the old town is the beating heart of Istanbul, marked by landmarks of incredible historical significance, making the place a haven for history buffs. And if you get tired of the leisurely exploration of the reminders of the city place as the center of power during the Ottoman and Byzantine empires — like the Topkapi Palace, the Blue Mosque, the Hagia Sophia, and other historic buildings and landmarks — you can head onto the traditional bazaars for a sneak peek into the local life.

The Bosphorus promenade is also perfect for leisurely and waterfront activities, and it is punctuated by numerous waterfront restaurants offering delicious meals and fabulous views from the side.

Unlike the city's outer districts, which, in the past decades, have gone through a series of renewals to cope with the fast-growing population, the old part of European Istanbul remains faithful to its traditional past, in forever remembrance of the magnificent bygone eras. It remains a truly European city center, focusing on tourism.

THE NEW PART OF ISTANBUL'S EUROPEAN SIDE

Developed in the 19th and 20th centuries, the newer part of the city's European side stands in contrast to the old town. North of the Golden Horn, you'll only find commercial areas, modern architecture, and broad avenues, all built at the tail end of the Ottoman Empire or after the rise of the Turkish Republic. Despite this, this area offers plenty of unique experiences to the visitors. You might not find landmarks with colorful history — but you can still experience the cultural significance of the shopping districts, restaurants, and entertainment venues.

Did You Know?

Besides the remnants of the ancient stone wall that once divided the old city (the Golden Horn Sea Wall of Constantinople), the Golden Horn also has a unique landmark that offers a glimpse into both sides of Istanbul at once. As its name implies, Miniaturk is a miniature version of everything Istanbul has to offer. From stunning architectural structures to natural beauties on both sides of the city, Miniaturk embodies diversity. It's an excellent option for those who, while staying on the European side, want to learn more about the Asian side, as well, but have a limited time during their visit.

MAIN ATTRACTIONS

Some of Istanbul's main attractions are on the city's European side. Whether you're interested in exploring art or history through the landmarks, learning about different cultures by visiting mosques and bazaars, or diving into the city's fabulous nightlife, you'll be able to have your fill at Istanbul's European side.

The central districts within the old part of the European side of Istanbul include Fatih, Sultanahmet, and Eminonu, all well-known tourist attractions.

SULTANAHMET

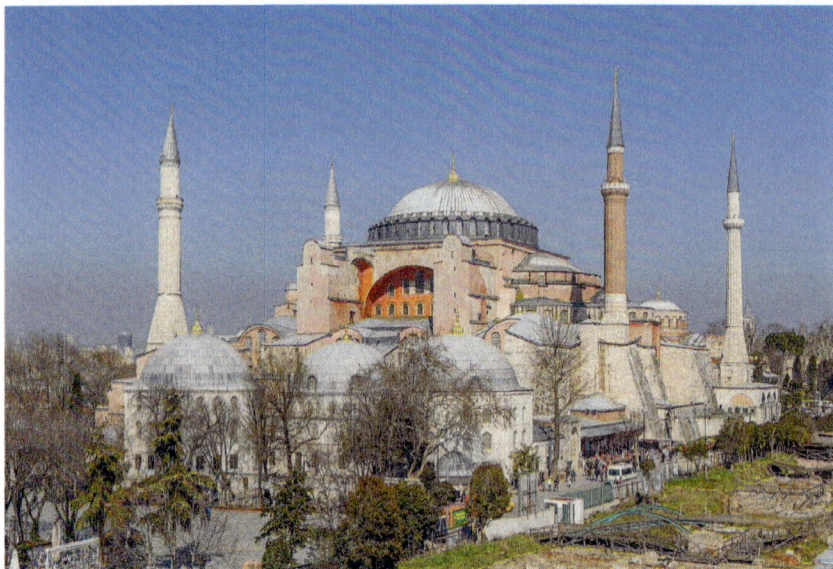

Hagia Sophia.[7]

The historic heart of Istanbul, Sultanahmet, is home to some of the city's most iconic landmarks, a few of which are included on UNESCO's World Heritage list. In this area, you can marvel at the grandeur of the Hagia Sophia, explore the Blue Mosque (also known as the Sultan Ahmed Mosque, and tour the Topkapi Palace and museum. You can also wander through the ancient Hippodrome and explore the depths of the Basilica Cistern.

Blue Mosque.[8]

As of the writing of this book, the Hagia Sophia is open from 9 AM to 7:30 PM every day, while the Blue Mosque is open from 9 AM to 6 PM. Keep in mind that for non-worshippers, the mosque is closed during prayer hours, which are around 6:20 AM, 6:37 AM, 1:29 PM, 4:15 PM, 6:35 PM, and 8:06 PM. However, please make sure to double-check the opening hours online should there be any slight changes to their schedule.

Hagia Sophia Address: Sultan Ahmet, Ayasofya Meydani No:1, 34122 Fatih/ Istanbul, Turkiye.

Blue Mosque Address: Binbirdirek, At Meydani Cd No:10, 34122 Fatih/Istanbul, Turkiye.

Topkapi Palace.[9]

As of the writing of this book, the opening hours for the Topkapi Palace are 10 AM to 4 PM, Wednesday to Monday, while on Tuesdays, the palace is closed to visitors. However, please make sure to double-check the opening hours online should there be any slight changes to their schedule.

Topkapi Palace Address: Cankurtaran, 34122 Fatih/Istanbul, Turkiye.

Basilica Cistern.[10]

As of the writing of this book, the Basilica Cistern is open from 9 AM to 10 PM every day, but due to the length of the tour (1.5-2 hours), the last entry is at 6:30 PM. However, please make sure to double-check the opening hours online should there be any slight changes to their schedule.

Basilica Cistern Address: Alemdar, Yerebatan Cd. 1/3, 34110 Fatih/ Istanbul, Turkiye.

Hippodrome of Istanbul.[11]

As of the writing of this book, you can visit the ancient Hippodrome every day all year round. Guided tours start at 9 AM Monday-Sunday. However, please make sure to double-check the opening hours online should there be any slight changes to their schedule.

Hippodrome Address: Binbirdirek, At Meydani Cd No:53 D:68, 34122 Fatih/ Istanbul, Turkiye.

Sultanahmet was the thriving center of the area many times throughout history. Among the historical relics of the area, you can find reminders of the Byzantine Empire, Constantinople, and the Ottoman Empire. Archaeological records also suggest that the foundation for the first settlements was placed right at the entry point of the Golden Horn about 7,000 years B.C. The first evidence of people inhabiting the place dates back to 667 B.C. One of the crucial points in history Sultanahmet provides a glimpse into are the foundations of Byzantion at Punta del Serraglio (where Topkapi Palace stands nowadays) by Byzas, the arrival of Constantine in 324 A.D., and the city's subsequent transport formation of the port town into the magnificent Constantinople, which then became the capital of the Roman Empire. The marks of the Ottoman religious power speak of different times, which began in 1453 when the city went under the rule of the Ottoman Empire. With all these changes

in its historical and cultural landscape, there is no wonder the Sultanahmet district is known as one of the must-see tourist attractions in Turkey and the entire world.

FATIH AND EMINONU

Valens Aqueduct.[12]

Named after Sultan Mehmed, the Ottoman ruler who seized control over Constantinople, Fatih is another old and highly-visited neighborhood in Istanbul's European side. Surrounding the Sultanahmet district, Fatih has plenty of historically significant attractions on its own, like the Valens Aqueduct or the Suleymaniye Mosque. Fatih is also home to the University of Istanbul.

Suleymaniye Mosque.[13]

As of the writing of this book, the Valens Aqueduct can be visited 24/7, while the Suleymaniye Mosque is open between 9 AM and 5:45 PM, except during prayer hours. However, please make sure to double-check the opening hours online should there be any slight changes to their schedule.

Valens Aqueduct Address: Kalenderhane, 34083, Fatih/Istanbul, Turkiye.

Suleymaniye Mosque Address: Suleymaniye, Prof. Siddik Sami Onar Cd. No:1, 34116 Fatih/Istanbul, Turkiye.

Galata Bridge.[14]

Eminonu showcases the historic Galata Bridge with its picturesque view of the Golden Horn area, a busy ferry port, and the equally buzzing Spice Bazaar. The latter is open from 9 AM to 7 PM every day except on public and religious holidays. However, please make sure to double-check the opening hours online should there be any slight changes to their schedule.

Spice Bazaar Address: Rustem Pasa, 34116 Fatih/Istanbul, Turkiye.

TAKSIM AND BEYOĞLU

Located on the new part of Istanbul's European side, Taksim and Beyoglu give you a glimpse into a mixture of historical heritage, contemporary architecture, and vibrant urban life.

Istiklal Avenue.[15]

With its main pedestrian street, Istiklal Avenue, Taksim serves as a focal point showcasing historical buildings, music venues, theaters, art galleries, and trendy shops — all punctuated by hotels, restaurants, and other avenues for leisurely activities. Beyoğlu, on the other hand, is well known for its arts and nightlife. With its narrow winding streets and European-style buildings, the area is the most similar to Sultanahmet in the old town. At the same time, it already has plenty of elements of modern architecture. It's known for the Galata neighborhood and its charming boho-chic atmosphere, which attracts those with an artistic, creative soul.

Istiklal Avenue Address: Istiklal Cd., Beyoglu/Istanbul, Turkiye.

OTHER ATTRACTIONS ON ISTANBUL'S EUROPEAN SIDE

BAKIRKÖY

If you're looking to escape the city rush and prefer a less touristy spot, Bakırköy will be your ideal place. While offering serene waterfront views, this coastal district also has plenty of action. Whether you want to partake in relaxing strolls along the promenade, visit the vast shopping centers where you can buy everything you can imagine, or relax in the green spaces of Atatürk Forest, you can do it in Bakırköy.

Bakırköy.[16]

ORTAKÖY

You can hardly get closer to the Bosphorus Strait while still on the European side of the city than by visiting Ortaköy. It's a highly popular spot among those looking for a perfect backdrop for photos, as the magnificent Bosphorus Bridge is just a stone's throw away. If you want to witness the picture-perfect little restaurants of Istanbul, Ortaköy is the place to be. A must-try is the baked potato, a local specialty, offered in almost all cafes and restaurants along the water. The district is also famous for art galleries and Sunday street markets. Most markets open at 8 or 9 AM and operate until 10 PM or midnight.

NİŞANTAŞI

This distinctively exclusive neighborhood is known for its high-end boutiques, luxurious dining prospects, and diverse art galleries and buildings boasting stunning Art Nouveau architecture. A recommended attraction to visit near Nişantaşı is the Istanbul Lütfi Kırdar Convention and Exhibition Center. The venue doesn't have fixed opening hours, and you can visit during specific events.

The Nişantaşı area is perfect for everyone looking to explore Istanbul's modern architectural and cultural history while enjoying the city's cosmopolitan vibes.

EYÜP SULTAN

A well-known pilgrimage site for Muslims, the Eyüp Sultan Mosque is situated in the Eyüp Sultan district. Make sure to visit the Pierre Loti Hill while you're in this neck of the woods. Besides enjoying a cup of traditional Turkish coffee or tea, you can also enjoy the breathtaking vistas of the Golden Horn. The district's old-world feel will charm you, while the calming spiritual aura will provide a much-needed break from the city.

Eyüp Sultan Mosque.[17]

As of the writing of this book, the Eyüp Sultan Mosque is open 24 hours daily except during prayer times. The Pierre Loti Hill is open from 9:00 AM to 11:00 PM every day. However, please make sure to double-check the opening hours online should there be any slight changes to their schedule.

Eyüp Sultan Mosque Address: Eyup Merkez, 34050 Eyupsultan/Istanbul, Turkiye.

Pierre Loti Hill Address: Eyup Merkez, Idris Kosku Cd., 34050 Eyupsultan/Istanbal, Turkiye.

SARIYER

Sarıyer district is located along the Bosphorus Strait and is the northernmost area of the European side. It's a slightly quieter district known for its seafood restaurants, historic mansions (known as yali), and beautiful natural vistas, including the stunning Belgrad Forest. While here, visit the Rumeli Fortress for a historical expedition, stroll the waterfront neighborhoods, admire its urban and suburban surroundings, and enjoy fresh seafood by the water.

Rumeli Fortress.[18]

As of the writing of this book, the fortress is open from 9 AM to 5 PM every day, except for Monday, during winter, and from 9 AM to 7 PM every day, except for Monday, during summer. However, please make sure to double-check the opening hours online should there be any slight changes to their schedule.

Rumeli Fortress Address: Rumeli Hisari, Yahya Kemal Cd., 34470 Sariyer/Istanbul, Turkiye.

TRANSPORT

The fastest and most efficient way to travel around the European side of Istanbul is by metro. Catch the M2 line runs, and it will take you from the Taksim Square area to the Haciosman district. An equally popular method for getting around is taking the tram. The T1 line covers the European side of Istanbul, operating between Bağcılar and Kabatas. It has stops in famous sites, including Karaköy, Sultanahmet, and Eminonu.

The European side of Istanbul is also covered by several bus lines connecting its busy neighborhoods, so this could also be a viable option, even if it is a little slower. Still, it's great for sightseeing.

If you are looking for a scenic transportation experience, visiting the coastal area, or traveling between the cities on the European and Asian sides or to the Princes' Islands, you can take the ferry.

If the weather becomes unfavorable, or you have a lot of bags with you, the most convenient option is to use a taxi. Make sure to agree with a driver on a fixed price beforehand, or use a metered taxi where you can know how much you pay ahead of the journey to avoid being overcharged.

Lastly, suppose you're doing a lot of sightseeing and landmark touring in the old town. In that case, walking will probably be the best way to ensure you don't miss anything. It also gives you the freedom to stop anywhere, anytime, whether it's for taking a picture, grabbing a snack, or anything else.

EXPERIENCES

Strolling through the Grand Bazaar market is a must-have experience for those looking for a taste of Istanbul's street food. If you're in the mood for shopping, you'll also find plenty of souvenirs here, including jewelry or traditional ceramics and textiles made by local artists. The market is open from 8:30 AM to 7 PM, Monday to Saturday.

If you're an art lover, the Istanbul Modern Museum in Karaköy will give you ample opportunity to appreciate the city's contemporary art scene. By touring it, you'll be able to admire the massive collection of art and exhibitions highlighting Istanbul's colorful cultural heritage. The museum welcomes visitors from 10 AM to 6 PM every day, except on Monday when it's closed.

Another way to explore the Turkish capital's historical and cultural background is strolling through Balat and Fener, where you'll see colorful houses and street art.

If you want to see more traditional art pieces of architectural landmarks, wander around the Galata Neighborhood. Make sure to try authentic Turkish coffee at one of the cafes on this historic street.

If you're looking to explore nature, covering the area of Gulhane Park is a must. The park got its name (Gulhane is a Persian term that means "house of roses"') from its vast green surroundings featuring flower arrangements. There is even a tulip festival in the spring, so check it out if you're visiting during this season. Besides the flowers, the park also offers a glimpse into the Ottoman architectural marvels, showcasing the cultural hallmarks of this defining period in the city's history. You can visit between 6 AM and 10:30 PM, seven days a week.

WHERE TO EAT

The streets of the Istanbul European side are carpeted with cafes and restaurants, offering a wide range of products and services catering to everyone's budget. Besides some of the most expensive places in Europe, you'll also find affordable options. The Ortaköy neighborhood is particularly famous for its eateries, often featuring plenty of open space in their surroundings and offering a spectacular view of the ferry port and the Bosphorus. You can't go wrong by choosing any of them.

Foodies will also appreciate the experience of trying the Balik Ekmek, a traditional Turkish fish sandwich you can get on the Galata Bridge. While enjoying food on the European side of Istanbul, you can tie your culinary experience with an activity like a boat tour on the Bosphorus. There is no better way to enjoy authentic Turkish seafood than getting on the water and munchkin while admiring the beautiful skyline and crossing from one continent to another.

SHOPPING GUIDE

If your main activity during a holiday is shopping, you can't miss a stroll among the high-end boutiques of Nisantasi. It might be a luxury shopping district, but it offers quality, providing a unique shopping experience.

The European side of Istanbul also has plenty of shopping malls where you can find everything you need and want at competitive prices.

Kanyon: Kanyon is located in Istanbul's most populated shopping district, Levent.

Address: Levent, Buyukdere Cd. No: 185, 34394 Sisli/Istanbul, Turkiye.

Metrocity: In the same area as Kanyon, you'll find Metrocity, a shopping mall featuring gourmet dining options, electronic stores, and a careful selection of fashion brands.

Address: Levent, Buyukdere Cd. No:171, 34330 Besiktas/Istanbul, Turkiye.

Zorlu Center: The Zorlu Center is another highly recommended place to visit. This shopping mall provides the full experience, offering stores, art, dining, and entertainment options.

Address: Levazim, Vadi Caddesi Zorlu Center No:2, 34340 Besiktas/Istanbul, Turkiye.

In Sisli, you'll find the city's largest shopping malls featuring stores, a cinema complex, an ice rink, an indoor roller coaster ride, and more. These malls are perfect for families who want an all-around shopping and entertainment experience.

In Bayrampasa, Forum Istanbul is another place catering to all ages. It houses the Legoland Discovery Center and the Sea Life Istanbul Aquarium.

Forum Istanbul Address: Kocatepe, Pasa Cd, 34045 Bayrampasa/Istanbul, Turkiye.

Mall of Istanbul: The Mall of Istanbul is located in Basaksehir. It features wide-ranging store options from international retailers to high-end brands and a highly popular food court.

Address: Ikitelli OSB, Suleyman Demirel Blv No:7, 34490 Basaksehir/Istanbul, Turkiye.

As of the writing of this book, the opening hours for all the malls are 10 AM - 10 PM every day. However, please make sure to double-check the opening hours online should there be any slight changes to their schedule.

ENTERTAINMENT

If you're looking for some fun and excitement in the European side of Istanbul, you'll likely find it in the newer part of the area. Here, all neighborhoods are packed with bars and nightclubs, where you can enjoy the nightlife, dance the night away, try out trendy cocktails, or get to know the locals.

ACCOMMODATIONS

Henna Hotel: If you're staying in the Sultanahmet area of the old city, the Henna Hotel is one of the most recommended options. Located in the heart of Istanbul's European side, this boutique hotel represents convenient yet affordable accommodation. Besides being just a stone's throw away from the Blue

Mosque and the famous Hagia Sophia, the Henna Hotel also features a great rooftop area with a view of these and other landmarks. It's the perfect place for taking pictures and a good value for your money.

Address: Cankurtaran, Akbiyik Cd, No:9, 34122 Fatih/Istanbul, Turkiye.

Ecole St. Pierre Hotel: If you prefer to be lodged in the Galata and Beyoğlu areas, the Ecole St. Pierre Hotel is situated right beside the Galata Tower. This chic hotel is another central location suitable for exploring the modern side of European Istanbul. Initially, it was a French primary school with a dash of Italian heritage, so it also offers a little insight into traditional European architecture. The hotel features a picturesque courtyard, and you can choose to stay in either a traditional or contemporary room.

Address: Bereketzade, Galata Kulesi Sk. No: 14 D:20, 34420 Beyoglu/ Istanbul, Turkiye.

Çırağan Palace Kempinski: If you are staying in Besiktas, the Çırağan Palace Kempinski will give you an unforgettable lodging experience. With its dreamy 17th-century architecture, this Ottoman place will make you feel like royalty. It's perfect for a romantic getaway or if you just want to pamper yourself, surrounded by luxury and style. The hotel has an infinity pool with a view of the Maiden's Tower, the Bosphorus Bridge, and the entire Bosphorus Strait.

Address: Yildiz, Ciragan Cd. No:32, 34349 Besiktas/Istanbul, Turkiye.

Did You Know?

Some of the remains of the ancient Byzantine city wall, which also doubled as a defense line in times of war, are still found inside Istanbul's buildings. The restaurant of Ecole St. Pierre Hotel happens to feature one of these wall pieces, which you can see up close while having your meal.

Bosphorus Palace Hotel: If you're looking for accommodations in the Uskudar-Kadikoy area, the Bosphorus Palace Hotel is one of the top recommendations. Located by the Bosphorus Strait, this restored historical hotel offers lavish rooms decorated in a Neo-Ottoman style and views of its beautiful gardens. Beyond the gardens, you can also have an overview of the entire European side of Istanbul and the Bosphorus Strait. Moreover, the hotel is just a short walk from the Beylerbeyi Historical Summer Palace, also known for its elegance and grandeur.

Address: Beylerbeyi, Yaliboyu Cd. No:64. 34676 Uskudar/Istanbul, Turkiye.

CHAPTER

4

THE ASIAN SIDE

While the European side of Istanbul has long been more popular among tourists, the Asian (or Anatolian) side of the city also has a lot to offer visitors. From historical landmarks to the charming little Turkish coffee shops, the part of Istanbul on the Eastern side of the Bosphorus will delight you just as much as the vibrant yet nostalgic European side. This chapter showcases the Asian side of Istanbul, highlighting its background, culture, main attractions, and everything else that makes it an integral part of the city.

HISTORICAL AND BACKGROUND INFORMATION

Lying east of the European side, the Bosphorus Straits separate the Asian side of Istanbul, yet it also represents a significant bridge between the two continents. Unlike the European side, which sits on the Balkan Peninsula, the Asian side lies on the Anatolian Peninsula (hence the name, Anatolian side). It is characterized by hilly terrain and residential areas built on slopes with scenic waterfront views.

The Asian side of Istanbul.[19]

The shores of the Asian side are lined with districts like Beykoz, Kalamis, Kuzguncuk, Cengelkoy, Umraniye, Bostanci, Salacak, Beylerbi, Kandilli, Kadıköy and Üsküdar. Except for the latter two (prominent tourist hotspots), the rest of them have a much calmer vibe, often preferred by repeat visitors looking for a respite from the busy streets flooded by tourists and those considering moving to the city.

Overall, the entire Asian section of the Turkish capital is more residential. Students and workers replace the masses of tourists lodging on the European side. Nonetheless, if you decide to visit this side, you'll be greeted with majestic historical landmarks, monuments, and extraordinary and well-preserved natural areas. On top of that, you'll get a chance to look into a more authentic life of the fascinating neighborhoods that, despite the area's rapid development, have maintained their traditional values and heritage.

The Anatolian part of Istanbul is a unique mesh of scenic beauty and traditional lifestyle. From this side of the Bosphorus, you can admire views of the Princes' Islands, the Marmara Sea, the Straits itself, and many other picturesque landmarks, offering a chance for the best pictures and a lifetime of memories.

On top of the breathtaking vistas, you'll be able to relax more as the neighborhoods are less congested (except for Kadıköy and Üsküdar, of course), making the place ideal for a leisurely, relaxing visit. However, if you're visiting with your family, you'll have plenty of opportunities for fun activities, too, from picnics to sports to outdoor exploration. This side of Istanbul has many preserved natural areas with beautiful green spaces and rich flora and fauna you can explore and observe.

MAIN ATTRACTIONS

The Asian part of Istanbul features many breathtaking panoramas, must-see historical attractions, culturally rich districts, and areas you can't miss. Below are a few suggestions to include in your itinerary.

Did You Know?

You can easily travel between the Asian and European sides by ferry or hop onto the Princes' Islands through the waterway while staying on the Asian side. Exploring the Bosphorus Straits landmarks is easiest to do by ferry.

BEYKOZ

Nestled along the Bosphorus Strait and just past Üsküdar, you'll find Beykoz, a lush, serene district known for its lush forests and historic mansions. While it's a residential area, it features many colorful designs and not just architectural masterpieces like the ancient homes built during the Ottoman Empire's glory days. While these are protected structures, the slowly evolving residential homes offer just as an interesting sight to marvel at, not to mention they're close to small restaurants where you can try the local delicacies while you sit and watch the locals go about their day. It's an ideal spot for those looking to escape the city's hustle and immerse themselves in nature.

Anadolu Hisari.[20]

A little further down, the Anadolu Hisarı Fortress offers a glimpse into the Ottoman past, and the Polonezköy Nature Park is perfect for hiking and picnics. With tight reign over the maritime traffic, Anadolu Hisarı served as an efficient military outpost and a successful defensive line of Constantinople from potential threats. The fortress reflects its era and purpose and showcases the best of Ottoman architecture. It has one main tower and five watchhtowers, all located on the Anatolian side of the Bosphorus. The historic building is open to the public, so you can stroll its grounds and admire the fortress itself. The surrounding area offers a view of the European side of Istanbul and the Bosphorus itself. There is also a neighborhood built around Anadolu Hisarı, which is known for its scenic charm, waterfront vistas, and historical houses.

Polonezköy Nature Park.[21]

As of the writing of this book, the Anadolu Hisarı Fortress is open every day from 10 AM to 6 PM. The Polonezköy Nature Park is open 24/7. However, the Anadolu Hisari Fortress is currently under restoration. Still, you can walk around it and marvel at it through its exterior walls. However, please make sure to double-check the opening hours online should there be any slight changes to their schedule.

Anadolu Hisarı Fortress Address: Anadolu Hisarı, 34810 Beykoz/Istanbul, Turkiye.

Polonezköy Nature Park Address: Polonez, 34986 Beykoz/Istanbul, Turkiye.

PENDIK

Housing the Istanbul Sabiha Gökçen International Airport, Pendik is a haven for those looking for a luxurious vacation adventure or even for a trip during a longer layover. Exploring the Pendik Marina, you can learn about the district's vast maritime history, or you can take to the water for some yachting and end your day with a seafront dining experience. To burn calories, you can walk on one of the walking paths or stroll through the parks in the coastal area.

SANCAKTEPE

With its rapidly expanding urban architecture, Sancaktepe is a district that combines modern residential areas with well-preserved natural scenery. Catering to a broad range of interests, the district has shopping malls (along with playgrounds and cinemas), cultural centers for entertainment, and plenty of hiking trails and views. Visit the Aydos Forest, and after a long hike to Aydos Hill, you'll be rewarded with a panoramic view of Istanbul, as if made for the perfect photo backdrop.

MALTEPE

Maltepe is the ideal destination for families and those seeking a quieter pace. It boasts vast green spaces like Maltepe Park and picturesque coastline promenades. Nature enthusiasts will appreciate the Orhangazi City Forest, while Bagdat Avenue offers a coastal retreat for shopping and dining enthusiasts.

As of the writing of this book, Maltepe Park is open every day between 10 AM and 10 PM. However, please make sure to double-check the opening hours online should there be any slight changes to their schedule.

Address: Cevizli, Tugay Yolu Cd. No:67, 34846 Maltepe/Istanbul, Turkiye.

Maltepe Mosque.[22]

The Maltepe Mosque is a stunning building with intricate details woven into its architectural designs. The traditional worship house, Gulsuyu Cemevi, is another cultural landmark worth visiting if you want to learn more about the local traditions and religion.

As of the writing of this book, the Maltepe Mosque is open 24/7, except for prayer hours. Gulsuyu Cemevi is also open 24 hours. However, please make sure to double-check the opening hours online should there be any slight changes to their schedule.

Maltepe Mosque Address: Feyzullah, Bagdat Cad. 346A, 34843 Maltepe/Istanbul, Turkiye.

Gulsuyu Cemevi Address: Gulsuyu, Adatepe Cd. No:18, 34848 Maltepe/Istanbul, Turkiye.

Maltepe Park.[23]

With its stunning views of the Marmara Sea and plenty of green spaces to explore, the Maltepe Sahil park is ideal for relaxing and unwinding. While you explore the grounds strolling the walkways, your children can play in one of

the playgrounds. Other parks in Maltepe you can explore are the Idealtepe Coast Park, which offers opportunities for outdoor sports and picnics for an all-around family day, and the Maltepe Sahil Park, the place made for scenic strolls and relaxation, with plenty of restaurants and cafes to visit. The park is open 24/7.

Address: Yali, Turgut Ozal Blv. No:223, 34844 Maltepe/Istanbul, Turkiye.

Exploring the Maltepe Organic Pazari is a fantastic way to immerse yourself in the local culture. With everything from fresh spices and products to hand-made crafts, the bustling market has a wide variety of goods and souvenirs to suit any pocket.

As of the writing of this book, the opening hours are as follows:

✦ *Monday, from 8 AM to 12 AM.*

✦ *Tuesday, from 8 AM to 10 AM, 12 PM to 1 PM, 3 PM to 4 PM, and 9 PM to 10 PM.*

✦ *Wednesday, from 8 AM to 9 AM, 1 PM to 4 PM, and 11 PM to 12 AM.*

✦ *Thursday, from 8 AM to 9 AM, 11 AM to 3 PM, and 8 PM to 9 PM.*

✦ *Friday, open 24 hours.*

✦ *Saturday, from 11 AM to 8 PM and from 10 PM to 11 PM.*

✦ *Sunday, from 9 AM to 8 PM.*

However, please make sure to double-check the opening hours online should there be any slight changes to their schedule.

Address: Kislali Cd. No:18, Maltepe/Istanbul, Turkiye.

ATAŞEHIR

Watergarden Istanbul.[24]

Ataşehir embodies the modern and exclusive vibe of Istanbul. The district is characterized by dapper residential towers and business centers, not to mention luxury shopping malls like Watergarden Istanbul, catering to every shopaholic's dream. For travelers seeking a blend of luxury living, high-end dining, and entertainment options, Ataşehir is the district to explore. If you're looking for a little excitement on the Asian side of Istanbul, you can experience the booming business district of Atasehir with its stunning views. Besides business centers, the district is also a haven for shopping lovers, with everything else Istanbul has to offer close by.

As of the writing of this book, the Watergarden Istanbul is open 10 AM - 10 PM every day. However, please make sure to double-check the opening hours online should there be any slight changes to their schedule.

Address: Barbaros, Kizilbegonya Sok 10/1, 34746 Atasehir/Istanbul, Turkiye.

TRANSPORT

Besides the ever-convenient ferries across the Bosphorus, Istanbul's Anatolian section is well connected to the Western side through several transportation options, including the Metrobus and the Marmaray metro lines. If you choose to use the ferry, the lines BUDO (Bursa Deniz Otobüsleri), Şehir Hatları, and İDO (İstanbul Deniz Otobüsleri) will be your go-to options for the European terminals. They have several lines operating from Kadıköy and Üsküdar. Besides the commuter ferries, you can also hop on a cruise tour ferry for a more relaxing, leisurely experience. Here, you can learn about the landmarks and buildings adorning the Bosphorus or on the islands of Burgazada, Heybeliada, and Buyukada, which are also popular ferry tour destinations for day trips from the Asian side.

Taking the Metrobus is another quick and convenient way to travel between the Asian and European sides of Istanbul. The Zincirlikuyu to Sogutlucesme line is the fastest route but can be congested during peak hours. The Marmaray train, operating between Kazlicesme (on the European side) and Üsküdar (on the Asian side), on the other hand, is always reliable as it travels under the Bosphorus, avoiding traffic jams.

Any cross-country bus line can also reach the Anatolian side of Istanbul. Your bus will arrive at the Üsküdar bus station, from where you can continue toward your destination in Istanbul. If you're staying mainly on the Asian side, arriving from the Sabiha Gokcen airport is recommended. Or, if you're commuting with a bus, use a route that connects to the Harem bus station.

Situated alongside the Marmaray tunnel, the Ayrılıkçeşme railway connects to the M4 Istanbul Metro, which you can use to explore the Asian side. Likewise, the ferry and bus terminals at the Bostancı transportation hub have several routes toward both sides of the Turkish capital, including a bus line connecting to the M4 Kadıköy-Kartal metro line, providing seamless access to all Asian districts.

While the best way to get around the Asian side alone is by using public transportation, some areas are best for exploring by walking or biking. The winding streets, hills, and slopes of the natural preservation sites are ideal for strolls. Some have hiking or jogging trails for the convenience of those who love to have an active vacation.

Riding the circular tram known as the Kadıköy Tram (or Kadıköy-Moda Nostalgic Tramway) provides another efficient mode of transportation

for getting around on the Asian side of Istanbul. Operating a single line over 1.6 miles between Kadıköy and Moda, the route has several stops in the Anatolian neighborhoods.

EXPERIENCES

To explore the masterpiece of authentic Anatolian architecture, check out the Kuzguncuk and Yeldeğirmeni areas.

YELDEĞIRMENI

Yeldeğirmeni is famous for its street art, including some of the most intricate murals you'll find in all of Turkey. Plus, the neighborhood is just a short trip away from Anadolu Hisari, making it perfect for combining a multifaceted itinerary with a day of relaxation from your city adventures. Bostancı, the district boasting recreational areas and parks with beautiful natural scenery along the coastline, is ideal for leisurely activities, enjoying the waterfront view, jogging, and other outdoor sports activities.

GOZTEPE

Istanbul Toy Museum.[25]

A great family activity could be visiting the Istanbul Toy Museum in the Goztepe district. This unique museum houses a collection of over 4,000 toys from different eras of toy-making history since the 18th century. Here, children can admire toys from different cultures and places across the globe, including Western-inspired vintage Barbie dolls, and also see classic Turkish toys to sneak a peek into the history of Turkish children's childhood.

As of the writing of this book, the Istanbul Toy Museum is open from 10 AM to 6 PM every day, except on Mondays when it's closed to visitors. However, please make sure to double-check the opening hours online should there be any slight changes to their schedule.

Address: Goztepe. Dr. Zeki Zeren Sk No:15, 34730 Kadikoy/Istanbul, Turkiye.

BEYKOZ

Visit Joshua's Hill in Beykoz and take in the wonderful view of the Anatolian shore of the Bosphorus. This hill is a shrine to Yusha and has a mosque and tomb dedicated to him that you can explore. This hill is 202 meters above sea level and is an important landmark for vessels coming from the Black Sea, which you may be able to see.

As of the writing of this book, you can visit at any time of the day, any day of the week. However, please make sure to double-check the opening hours online should there be any slight changes to their schedule.

Address: Anadolu Kavagi, 34825 Beykoz/Istanbul, Turkiye.

Did You Know?

Numerous Turkish soap operas were filmed in the Kuzguncuk neighborhood, which features traditional Ottoman houses known as yali.

WHERE TO EAT

While Kadıköy is probably the most famous district for delicious culinary experiences, other districts also offer a diverse selection of products and services, including trendy cafes with modern snacks, international restaurants, and, of course, the best of traditional Turkish cuisine for an all-around experience. Try as many types of kebabs and seafood dishes as you can, as these are all sourced from local and fresh ingredients. The traditional Turkish breakfast of olives, cheeses, tomatoes, pastries, and last but not least, aromatic Turkish coffee (a brew much stronger than black coffee in modern coffee shops) is another great recommendation for visitors to the Asian

side of Istanbul. If you're looking for something more substantial to refuel yourself after sightseeing, try lahmacun (a round, thin dough with minced meat and spices on top) or pide (a flatbread akin to pizza). Taste manti, Turkish dumplings traditionally filled with cheese or meat and eaten with yogurt and garlic on the side, or try a Turkish delight, baklava, and other local desserts.

If you prefer to eat on the go, popular street foods like kokoreç (spiced lamb sandwich), midyear dolma (stuffed mussels), and simit (bread rings covered with sesame seeds) are plentiful and filling. Maltepe district, in particular, has a vibrant street food scene (along with plenty of restaurants to suit all budgets and tastes).

Karadeniz Pide Kebap Salonu: Karadeniz Pide Kebap Salonu serves casual and modern plates and traditional Turkish dishes like kebabs and pide (Turkish pizza) in a welcoming atmosphere.

As of the writing of this book, the opening hours for Karadeniz Pide & Kebap Salonu are 9 AM to 9 PM every day. However, please make sure to double-check the opening hours online should there be any slight changes to their schedule.

Address: Icerenkoy, Eski Uskudar Yolu Caddesi No:58, 34752 Atasehir/Istanbul, Turkiye.

Ceviz Ağacı Cafe & Restaurant: Ceviz Ağacı Cafe & Restaurant (also in the Maltepe area) is another fantastic option for those seeking an unforgettable dining experience with a view on the side. As one of the coastline establishments in Maltepe, the restaurant guarantees picturesque vistas of the Marmara Sea. Great panorama notwithstanding, the menu won't leave you disappointed either, especially if you love seafood. You can also try the traditional Turkish meze or spend the evening sipping a drink or two at the bar while enjoying the scenery.

As of the writing of this book, the opening hours for Ceviz Ağacı Cafe & Restaurant are every day from 6 AM - 12 AM. However, please make sure to double-check the opening hours online should there be any slight changes to their schedule.

Address: Kosuyolu, Muhittin Ustundag Cd. No:85, 34718 Kadikoy/Istanbul, Turkiye.

Istanbul has plenty of restaurants catering to the lovers of Asian cuisine. You'll find tasty Japanese dishes like ramen, sushi rolls, or tempura, and you can wash these down with sake for an authentic Japanese-style eating experience.

SHOPPING GUIDE

The Asian side of Istanbul has a wide range of shopping malls, including Akasya, Palladium, Maltepe Park, and Kozzy, and markets selling everything you can think of, so if anywhere you want to spend money in the Anatolian districts, you'll have ample places to do so.

Bagdat Avenue: Bagdat Avenue, or Bağdat Caddesi, is considered the most popular shopping avenue on the Asian side of Istanbul. There, you'll find luxurious department stores, high-end boutiques, and trendy cafes to enjoy a cup of coffee and delicious dessert after a long day of shopping. If you're a shopaholic, this avenue is a must-visit for a fun shopping spree.

Covering the neighborhoods of Altintepe Bostanici, Maltepe, and Cevizli, Bagdat Avenue in Bostanci has also been likened to Rodeo Drive by travel writers due to its numerous shopping centers and high-end luxury boutiques.

Maltepe Mall: With its variety of shops, food court, and movie theater, Maltepe Mall is a shopaholic's haven and a wonderful spot to relax and grab a bite after sightseeing.

As of the writing of this book, Maltepe Mall is open every day from 10 AM to 10 PM. However, please make sure to double-check the opening hours online should there be any slight changes to their schedule.

Address: Cevizli, Tugay Yolu Cd. No:67, 34846 Maltepe/Istanbul, Turkiye.

SPORTS AND LEISURE

The most popular sports on Istanbul's Asian side are jogging, hiking, and skating — at least judging by the number of trails and skateparks located in the area.

Ataşehir Skatepark: Ataşehir Skatepark is situated near the city's busiest, mostly densely populated districts, Kadıköy, Beykoz, and Çekmeköy, and is easily approachable from the TEM (E-80) highway. People of all ages like to gather here, showing their skills and socializing. There are also regular skate shows where professional skaters demonstrate their moves along with a visually appealing light show. Whether you're into skating or just in for the show, visiting the park can be an excellent opportunity to learn how the locals have fun and immerse yourself in part of their culture.

Address: Atasehir Ataturk, 34758 Atasehir/Istanbul, Turkiye.

Maltepe Skatepark: Located at the former Süreyya Beach on the Anatolian side, the Maltepe Skatepark is popular for skaters on both sides of Istanbul. You can easily reach it via the Marmaray bus by existing at the Süreyya Paşa stop. As the largest skatepark in the city (and they are all quite sizable), Maltepe Skatepark has everything you need for an adrenaline-packed adventure. It has plenty of tracks and ramps, not to mention convenient places to refill your energy with delicious food.

Address: Yali, 34844 Maltepe/Istanbul, Turkiye.

Ümraniye Tantavi Skateboard Park: If you're looking for an active day with your family, Ümraniye Tantavi Skateboard Park is a highly recommended place to visit. Children and everyone young at heart can try skating in the park's beginner-friendly wooden tracks. Or, if you prefer to stay on two wheels, you can arrive on a bicycle and take a tour. The locals often arrive on scooters and roller skates as well.

Address: Tantavi, 34764 Umraniye, Turkiye.

As of the writing of this book, all three skateparks are open 24/7. However, please make sure to double-check the opening hours online should there be any slight changes to their schedule.

ACCOMMODATIONS

If you're staying in the Maltepe district, explore Istanbul knowing that after a long day of sightseeing, you'll enjoy all the contemporary comforts at Days Hotel by Wyndham Istanbul. The hotel is located near the Istanbul Airport and the Istanbul Sabiha Gokcen Airport. It is close to several shopping malls and famous landmarks. Metro stations connecting to Sultanahmet, Taksim, and Kadıköy districts are also within walking distance.

Ebrus'Un Konagi Hotel Istanbul: Situated on Istanbul's Anatolian Side and offering a restaurant, daily buffet breakfast, meeting room, and conference hall, Ebrus'Un Konagi Hotel Istanbul is ideal for long-term guests. Here, you can indulge in a luxurious holiday featuring self-catering suites with island and sea views. Forty-two spacious rooms are beautifully decorated, complimenting the hotel's decor scheme of a combination of Italian-imported materials and modern Turkish architecture.

Address: Elifce Sk. No:3, Zumrutevler, Istanbul, Turkiye.

Radisson Blu Hotel: At the Radisson Blu Hotel, you can immerse yourself in the vibrant atmosphere of the Atasehir district, just a stone's throw away from the financial hub. Explore the city's cultural landmarks, including the famous Hagia Sophia and Blue Mosque. Relax in style, enjoy Turkish dishes at the Core Grill, and indulge in spa treatments. This hotel offers the perfect blend of business and leisure.

Address: Ataturk Mahallesi, Yakut Cd., 34758 Atasehir/Istanbul, Turkiye.

CHAPTER

5
THE PRINCES ISLANDS

The Princes Islands are the perfect spot to have a quiet pause amidst your exploration of the buzzing capital of Turkey, Istanbul. The archipelago is a beautiful natural area, combining enchanting views, an exciting history, and some fun and creative activities. They are the perfect location to unplug and detach yourself from the digital world and enjoy the abundance mother nature has to offer, from beaches to forests, as well as delicious food choices.

HISTORICAL/BACKGROUND INFORMATION

Adalar is the name the Turks call the Princes Islands. They exist about 12.5 miles off the coast of Istanbul, southeast of the Bosphorus, in the Marmara Sea. There are nine islands in total, with four inhabited with a population of less than 15,000. They are Büyükada (the largest Island), Heybeliada, Burguzada, Kinaliada (the other three inhabited ones), Sedef, Yassiada, Taysan, Kasik, and Siyriada (Private Islands owned by a select few who built homes there).

Princes Islands.[26]

During the Byzantine Empire, these clusters of Islands were used for purposes other than entertaining tourists. They were prisons for exile and homes for humiliated and disgraced members of the aristocratic community. Several Byzantine empresses resided in the convent of Buyukada during their exile.

Those prisoners or exiles were not treated as one would expect. They were people who had been accustomed to a specific lifestyle, which was maintained during their punishment. Instead of metal shackles, they lived in magnificently built mansions. They had the privilege of waking up to wondrous views every morning.

During the Ottoman Empire and especially in the 19th century, the rich and upper class of Istanbul began using the Islands as their resorts. They started constructing lavish wooden houses to accommodate their lifestyles. At the time, the communities that made up the Islands were so diverse they included Jewish, Armenian, and Greek ethnicities.

Did You Know?

Leon Trotsky, the Bolshevik leader, sought refuge in the Islands after Stalin expelled him from the USSR.

TRANSPORT

The way to get to the Islands is fairly straightforward for all four of them: Büyükada, Heybeliada, Burguzada, and Kinaliada. Two types of ferries can take you there: regular passenger ferries and fast passenger ferries (Sea Buses). These buses depart from more than one port in Istanbul, including Sirkeci, Kabatas, Eminonu, Yasilkoy, Besiktas, and Bostanci districts. Depending on the port you choose, the trip can take anywhere between 30 minutes and 75 minutes to reach the largest Island, Büyükada. A one-way ticket is 16TL per person at the time of writing. Be sure to check the ferry schedules, as they vary by season, and arrive early at the dock before the trip.

BÜYÜKADA

The name Büyükada means "big Island" in Turkish. As described by its name, the Island is the biggest of all the Princes Islands, spanning a little over two square miles. It is also the most popular for its beautiful beaches, monuments, and natural

sites, along with a variety of activities available for all ages.

HISTORICAL/BACKGROUND INFORMATION

The largest Island in the cluster was a place of exile for criminals and a spiritual living quarter during Byzantine times. Emperor Justin II ordered a palace and a monastery built in 569 CE. This was the first religious building of many to come, serving as both a place of worship and exile quarters for empresses and emperors.

The Island served as the exile home for Leon Trotsky in 1929. During his four years there, he wrote his autobiography and The History of the Russian Revolution.

Did You Know?

In 2015, the mansion Trotsky stayed in was put on sale for 4.4 million dollars.

MAIN ATTRACTIONS

There are several interesting pit stops on the Island:

The Historic Wooden Houses: The Island is home to several historic wooden houses, some of which could easily date back more than

300 years. The Turks call these houses Kosku. At the height of Ottoman rule, several aristocrats built magnificent villas to spend the hotter days of the year in. These were also called resort houses. While you can't exactly enter the houses, since they are private property now, you can enjoy the views of the building and gardens from the outside. While walking down the streets, take a minute to snap some beautiful pictures of these intricately built constructs.

Adalar Museum: This is a must-see site for all the history lovers. The museum introduces you to the story of the princes' islands from their inception until the modern day. The museum houses many artifacts depicting the history of the island and the people who resided there.

Adalar Museum.[27]

As of the writing of this book, the opening hours are Tuesday to Sunday, from 10:30 AM until 5:00 pm. The site closes on Mondays, and the ticket costs 20 TL per person. However, please make sure to double-check the opening hours online should there be any slight changes to their schedule.

Address: Aya Nikola Mevkii, Buyukada, 34970 Adalar/Istanbul, Turkiye.

The Old Greek Orphanage: Named as one of the largest wooden buildings in Europe. The site, which is mostly in ruins now, was initially built as a casino and hotel in the late 19th century. However, these plans never came to fruition. Later on, Eleni Zarifi, a Greek citizen, converted the building into an orphan-age with over 200 beds, a library, a dining hall, and a theater. The second you

see it, you'll get the vibes of beholding a magical castle out of the mists of time. Unfortunately, the orphanage went out of business in 1964. While visitors are not allowed inside the building, if you do decide to go up the hill to see it, you'll be rewarded with a wonderful view of the Marmara Sea.

The Old Greek Orphanage.[28]

Address: Buyukuda – Maden Mh, Carkifelek cd, 91/1, 34970 Adalar/Istanbul, Turkiye.

Monastery of St. George Koudounas: Sources suggest that the building on top of the Yuce Tepe hill was built in 963 during the reign of Nicephorus II Phocas. Aside from the gorgeous view you'll see once you get to the top, you'll be treated to one of the islands' historical gems. You can put in a little exercise by walking up the kilometer-long cobblestone path after driving up in an electric vehicle or riding a bike.

As of the writing of this book, there is no clear documentation of the monastery's opening hours, though some suggest that visiting hours are permitted from the early morning until around 7 pm. However, please make sure to double-check the opening hours online should there be any slight changes to their schedule.

The Old Town Center: The oldest and main square on the island is called Iskele Meydani, or the Dock Square. The area teems with some of the best restaurants, cafes, and delicious dondurma vendors (ice cream).

Aya Yorgi Church: Initially called the Agios Georgios Greek Orthodox Monastery. The site was built by St George in 1751. The church has a beautiful story tied to it. Apparently, during the Byzantine era, during the occupation, the priests buried the St George icon among other relics for safekeeping. Years pass, and Aya Yorgi dreams of a shepherd telling him to dig. Following the instructions given to him in his dream, he found the lost treasures.

Aya Yorgi Church.[29]

As of the writing of this book, the opening hours for the Aya Yorgi Church are between 10 AM to 4 PM all week long. However, please make sure to double-check the opening hours online should there be any slight changes to their schedule.

Address: Nizam, Insel Buyukada, 34970 Adalar/Istanbul, Turkiye.

Other: You should consider heading to many other interesting sites once you're on the island. For example, there is the Hristos church, or the Hamidiye mosque, commissioned by Sultan Abdulhamit II.

TRANSPORT

Motor vehicles are not allowed on any of the Princes Islands. You can hop on an electric bus or taxi a couple of blocks from the main square or rent a bike to work those calves. You'll find several rental shops available the minute you step off the ferry when you arrive.

FAMILY FUN

The Islands are not just a historic and scenic destination. They include several beaches where you can relax and enjoy a quick dip or a relaxing sun tan. Some of the better-known beaches include Yorukali Beach, one of the more family-focused destinations known as the sandiest beach. Nakibey Plaji is also a family-friendly beach with a buffet restaurant. Halik Koyu is the biggest, cleanest, and most convenient beach, with restaurants, showers, sunbeds, and umbrellas available.

WHERE TO EAT

The archipelago is known for its fresh fish and restaurants that cook them in the most tasteful ways. If you're not a fish person, you'll become one there. Many quaint spots offer traditional dishes with a seafood twist.

The Prinkipo Meyhanesi Restaurant: The Prinkipo Meyhanesi Restaurant is a beautiful venue that offers live music on Fridays and Saturdays.
Address: Maden Mahallesi, Gulistan Cd. No:11, 34970 Adalar/Istanbul, Turkiye.

Yucetepe Kir Gazinosu: If you're looking for a meal with a view, head up to the Yucetepe Kir Gazinosu, on the Aya Yorgi hill, by the monastery.
Address: Nizam, Buyukada-nizam Mh., 34970 Adalar/Istanbul, Turkiye.

Eskibag Teras: Another great restaurant with a view is the Eskibag Teras, built on a cliff top.
Address: Nizam, Adalar, 34970 Adalar/Istanbul, Turkiye.

Buyuk ada Pasranesi: After a well-deserved meal, you'll need dessert, so get yourself to the Buyuk ada Pasranesi and enjoy the traditional Turkish tea and Turkish

delight. Don't forget to stop for some unforgettable dondurma (ice cream) in the main square.

Address: Buyukada – Maden, Sht. Recep Koc Cd. No:16. 34970 Adalar/Istanbul, Turkiye.

SHOPPING GUIDE

The Island's main square is the perfect spot for shopping. The local markets sell traditional souvenirs, jewelry, ceramics, and textiles. Street vendors also offer an opportunity to buy one-of-a-kind accessories and souvenirs.

ENTERTAINMENT

The Island hosts several cultural events throughout the year, so be sure to check the local events calendar for any festivals, music concerts, or exhibitions during your stay.

SPORTS AND LEISURE

The Island is known for its hiking trails. The best one is the circular hiking route, climbing the Aya Yorgi hill, which takes you through the main pit stops and attractions. From a starting point at the old clock tower in the market square, you'll pass the Neo-Gothic Catholic church of San Pacifico. You'll get to stop

by the Hamidiye mosque. You can rest in the middle, grab a bite in the Luna theme park, and then carry on towards the Aya Yorgi. On your way down, you can stop by Trotsky's renowned house and the Armenian church of Surp Asdvadzadzin.

ACCOMMODATIONS

Here are some of the best-recommended stays in Buyukada:

- ✦ **Aya Nikola Boutique Hotel** (*Address: Buyukada – Maden, Ayanikola Mevkii, Yilmaz Turk Cd. No:181, 34970 Adalar/Istanbul, Turkiye*).

- ✦ **Cenar Konak** (*Address: Nizam, Cinar Cd. No:9, 34970 Adalar/Istanbul, Turkiye*).

- ✦ **Ada Palas Hotel Buyukada** (*Address: Maden Mahallesi, Cicekliyali Sokak No:24, 34970 Buyukada/Istanbul, Turkiye*).

- ✦ **Splendid Palace Hotel** (*Address: Nizam, Yirmiuc Nisan Cd. No: 39, 34970 Adalar/Istanbul, Turkiye*).

- ✦ **Mavi Palas** (*Address: Nizam, Sht. Recep Koc Cd. No:4/A, 34970 Adalar/Istanbul, Turkiye*).

HEYBELIADA

The name Heybeli means "saddlebag" in Turkish, which is a metaphor for the island's geography. Heybeliada is the second biggest island among the Princes Islands and is also known as the greenest one. Some of its well-known features are her four hills, Degirmentepe, Umit Hill, Tasocagi, and Makarios Hills. The highest of them is Degirmentepe, which reaches a height of 136 meters. Followed closely by Umit Hill, home of the famous Heybeliada Seminary, also known as Priest Hill, at 85 meters high.

HISTORICAL/BACKGROUND INFORMATION

One of the well-known tidbits about the island is that it was where the famous Naval Cadet school was located. The school is located on the left side of the jetty, right as you exit the ferry. It holds within it the structure of the last surviving Eastern Roman church, Kamariotissa.

Did You Know?

Heybeliada is often called Halki, which means "copper in" Greek, referencing its antique copper mines.

HALKI SEMINARY

Halki Seminary.[30]

Halki Seminary (Holy Trinity) is located on the Northern hill. The seminary was active up until the conflict with Cyprus in 1971. The construction is well preserved and maintained, and two priests on premises serve daily in the Cathedral church.

As of the writing of this book, the Halki Seminary is open every day from 9 AM to 12:30 PM. However, please make sure to double-check the opening hours online should there be any slight changes to their schedule.

Address: Heybeliada, Adalar No:45, 34973 Adalar/Istanbul, Turkiye.

HEYBELIADA NAVAL HIGH SCHOOL

Heybeliada Naval High School.[31]

Heybeliada Naval High School (Bahirye) is probably the first building you'll see when getting closer to the island by sea. The school was founded in 1773 at Kasimpasa Shipyard. It was then called the School of Naval Engineering or Muhendishane i Bahr i Humayun. The building is open for visitors who wish to immerse themselves in the island's history.

Address: Heybeliada, 34973 Adalar / Heybeliada/Adalar/Istanbul, Turkiye.

HEYBELIADA SANATORIUM

Heybeliada Sanatorium.[32]

Heybeliada Sanatorium is another location you should check out. The out-doors is open to the public. In the old days, sanatoriums were hospital-like structures that treated mainly tuberculosis. The establishment was built in 1924 and since had several big names cared for in it, like the poet Ece Ayhan, the statesman Ismet Inonu, and the writer Rifat Ilgaz.

Address: Liman, Heybeliada Mahallesi, 34973 Adalar/Istanbul, Turkiye.

BET YAAKOV SYNAGOGUE

Bet Yaakov Synagogue.[33]

Bet Yaakov Synagogue, which the Neve Shalom Foundation built. The building was opened for worshippers in 1956. Today, it can be visited on Saturdays and other religious holidays.

Address: Heybeliada, Orhan Sk. No:8, 34973 Adalar/Istanbul, Turkiye.

HAGIOS NIKOLAOS CHURCH

Hagios Nikolaos Church was built by architect Stefanis Gaitanakis in 1857. It is said to have been built upon the ruins of a Byzantine church dedicated to St Nicholas, the patron saint of the mariners. The church is still open to worshippers after being restored with the permission of Abdulhamid II following a devastating earthquake in 1894.

As of the writing of this book, the church is said to be open to visitors wishing to worship during worship hours. However, please make sure to double-check the opening hours online should there be any slight changes to their schedule.

Address: Heybeliada, Imrali Sk. No:11, 34973 Adalar/Istanbul, Turkiye.

Did You Know?

Huseyin Rahmi Gurpinar, a well-known Turkish writer, lived on the island. His house has been converted into a museum and is open to visitors.

TRANSPORT

Like its bigger sister, no motor vehicles are allowed on the island. Most tours are done via electric vehicles. There are two main routes to go around the island: the Big tour and the small tour, also known as the Lovers tour.

FAMILY FUN

There are several family-friendly beaches where you can relax or have fun small activities with your family.

The Ada Beach Club: The Ada Beach Club on Cam Limani Bay has a one-of-a-kind backdrop of prolific rain forests. The beach has both sandy and grassy locations and includes activities like mini golf and a beach volleyball court.

Address: Camlik, Mevki, 34973 Adalar/Istanbul, Turkiye.

The Aqua Green Beach: The Aqua Green Beach is great for families, as it has the option of enjoying an aquapark as well as the beach. You can easily reach it from the pier via free transportation.

Address: Heybeliada, 34973 Adalar/Istanbul, Turkiye.

WHERE TO EAT

The variety of food on the island is not as vast as on Buyukada. However, you can easily find delicious dishes at any of the waterfront restaurants and cafes. The cuisines include Turkish mezes and seafood dishes. The Nazligul pudding shop is a main stop for life-changing, delectable pastries.

SHOPPING GUIDE

The island has many local stores that offer homemade artifacts and trinkets. You can easily find small souvenirs, textiles, and locally sourced foods like olives.

ENTERTAINMENT

There are concerts hosted on the Island during the summer. A naval band also tours the island during the annual Independence Day march.

BURGAZADA

Burgazada, or Burgaz as the locals call it, is the third island on the list in order of size. The word Burgazada means island fortress in Turkish. The island is known for its pebbled beaches, romantic setting, and historic and beautiful sites.

HISTORICAL/ BACKGROUND INFORMATION

Initially, Burgazada was home to the Greeks until the 1950s, when the Jewish families arrived and settled on the island, building many striking homes. In 1928, the island was where the first Sanatorium in Turkey was built.

MAIN ATTRACTIONS

Among the main places to visit are:

Aya Yani Church was built around 867. The church was erected in the historic area of the island and is a must-see. It is only a few minutes away from the ferry terminal. Over the years, the church has been restored on many occasions, the last of which was in 1896.

As of the writing of this book, Aya Yani Church is open every day of the week between 8.30 AM and 4 PM, except for Sundays between 9 AM and 12.15 PM, since it is the time of worship. However, please make sure to double-check the opening hours online should there be any slight changes to their schedule.

Address: Burgazada, Takimaga Meydani Sk., 34975 Adalar/Istanbul, Turkiye.

Did You Know?

It is said that priest Methodius was imprisoned in the dungeon located 11 steps in the underground area of the church. Later, he became a minister at the same church.

+ *The island is also home to the Bayrakli Monastery, located on top of a hill with sublime views.*

+ *The Museum of Sait Faik, a famous Turkish writer, is another must-see site on the island. The writer and poet lived and was inspired by the island. If you head out to his favorite restaurant, Kalpazankaya, you'll be greeted with his bronze statue.*

The Museum is open all days of the week except for Monday, from 10:30 AM until 4:30 pm.

TRANSPORT

Like the rest of the islands, Burgazada does not allow motorized vehicles. The island is only around 1.2 miles long, so you can cover the whole area on foot. Other alternatives are bike or horse-pulled carriages.

FAMILY FUN

Explore the beautiful island starting from the small Burgazada square, right off the ferry terminal. Either take a right to tour the small quaint space or head up any of the smaller streets to get to the Aya Yani Greek church. You'll probably be able to spot its dome from far away.

You can also hike to the highest point on the island, Hristos Hill. The hill is also home to the Monastery of Christ.

If you're tired of walking, renting a bike to get around faster and easier is possible.

You can also enjoy the beaches on the island. Just make sure to bring along your swim shoes. Some of these beaches have pebbles that may hurt your feet. Among those beaches are Halk Beach, Mimi Koy, Kalpazankaya Beach, and Camakya Aile Plaji.

WHERE TO EAT

Four Letter Word Coffee Café: If you're looking for modern choices and delicious options, head to the Four Letter Word Coffee cafe. This place is popular among the tourists and the locals.

Address: Burgazada, Takimaga Meydani Sk. No:3/A, 34975 Burgazada/Istanbul, Turkiye.

Burgazada Terrace Café: There is also the Burgazada Terrace cafe by the waterfront, offering your Turkish breakfast with a view.

Address: Burgazada, 35, Gezinti Yolu Cd., 34975 Adalar/Istanbul, Turkiye.

Ergun Patisserie: There is also Ergun Patisserie and cafeteria, right as you exit the ferry terminal, among other restaurants. They offer burek, manti (mini dumplings), and traditional Turkish tea.

Address: Burgazada Gezinti Yolu Cad., 34975 Burgazada/Istanbul, Turkiye.

Cennet Bahcesi Paradisos Café: The Cennet Bahcesi Paradisos cafe is perfect for a quiet meal with a view.

Address: Burgaza, No:60, Gonullu Cd. Ram Vakif Evleri No:60, 34975 Adalar/Istanbul, Turkiye.

Restaurant options include Barba Yani, Indos Pub, Anjelik Cafe, and Yasemin Restaurant.

SHOPPING GUIDE

Many of the local shops offer souvenirs and locally made products.

ACCOMMODATIONS

If you wish to extend your stay and explore the island further, here are the best recommendations for hotels:

+ **Villa Andrea** (Address: Burgazada, Yeni Kuyu Sk. No:3, 34975 Adalar/Istanbul, Turkiye).

+ **Pyrgos Hotel** (Address: Burgazada, Gezinti Yolu Cd. No:45, 34975 Burgazada/ Istanbul, Turkiye).

+ **Mehtap 45 Boutique Hotel** (Address: Burgazada, Mehtap Sk. No:47, 34975 Adalar/ Istanbul, Turkiye).

KINALIADA

It is the fourth largest island among the Prince's Islands and the closest to Istanbul, spanning less than a mile. The highest point within the island is Cinartepe which is 115 meters high. The name Kinaliada means henna, which is a reference to its reddish nature due to copper and iron deposits and vegetation.

HISTORICAL/ BACKGROUND INFORMATION

Also known as Kinali, the island has been home to many cultures, mainly Armenians.

Did You Know?

Romanos IV Diogenes was exiled to Kinaliada following his defeat at the hands of the Turkish leader Alparslan. The monastery where he resided during his exile is still standing today.

MAIN ATTRACTIONS

There are a few intriguing sites on the island, including:

The Monastery of Transfiguration: The Monastery of Transfiguration, located on the island's tip, has served Constantinople's Rum Orthodox community since the Eastern Roman Empire.

Address: Manastir Cd., 34035 Kinaliada/Istanbul, Turkiye.

Kinaliada Mosque: Kinaliada Mosque was built in 1964 and is unique with its asymmetrical triangular roof and modern design.

Kinaliada Mosque.[34]

Address: Kinaliada, Kinali Carsi Cd. No:15, 34977 Adalar/Istanbul, Turkiye.

TRANSPORT

Like the other islands, no motor vehicles are allowed.

FAMILY FUN

There are a few activities to entertain you and your family, including the beaches.

Kamo's Beach Club: Kamo's Beach Club is highly recommended on the other side of the island. You can hike your way there, but be careful; it's a steep climb, and the way down is littered with pebbles.

Address: Kinaliada, Kinali Carsi Cd. No:89, 34977 Adalar/Istanbul, Turkiye.

Teos Beach Club: There is also Teos Beach club. The club has a restaurant serving traditional Turkish breakfasts and dinners.

Address: Kinaliada, Kinali Carsi Cd. No:63, 34977 Adalar/Istanbul, Turkiye.

Kinaliada Iskele Beach: You can also head to the Kinaliada Iskele Beach. It is the easiest beach to find, with no entry fee. However, you will have to pay for a parasol and lounger. It also has a restaurant. The downside would be that it will be more crowded than most due to its accessibility.

Address: Kinaliada, 34977 Adalar/ Istanbul, Turkiye.

Kumluk Beach: There is also Kumluk Beach, a private property that charges an entrance fee. This beach has lifeguards and doctors and doesn't allow male-only groups.

Address: Fazil Ahmet Aykac Sokak 35 Kinali Ada, 34977 Adalar/Istanbul, Turkiye.

WHERE TO EAT

Teos Kinaliada Beach and Restaurant is among the many recommended options on the island. There is also the Proti Restoran.

You can't eat without enjoying ice cream after your meal, so make sure to get to Yesil Roma Dondurmasi after dinner.

For breakfast, be sure to check out Bahar Patisserie.

Teos Kinaliana Beach and Restaurant Address: Kinaliada, Kinali Carsi Cd. No:63, 34977 Adalar/Istanbul, Turkiye.

Proti Restoran Address: Kinaliana, Alsancak Cd. No:21/A, 34927 Adalar/Istanbul, Turkiye.

Yesil Roma Dondurmasi Address: Kinaliada, Kinali Carsi Cd. No:8/1, 34977 Adalar/Istanbul, Turkiye.

SHOPPING GUIDE

Several local shops offer locally sourced goods and handmade souvenirs and crafts.

ACCOMMODATIONS

The island includes a few boutiques and clean hostels for those who wish to stay longer.

6

TOURIST HOTSPOTS: KADIKOY AND USKUDAR

Kadıköy and Üsküdar are two prominent districts on the Asian side of Istanbul, Turkey. These areas have a rich historical significance and cultural heritage, enhancing the diversity of Istanbul. Both areas showcase a captivating blend of ancient historical landmarks and modern marvels, creating a dynamic energy of contemporary life.

Kadıköy and Üsküdar on the map.[35]

BRIEF HISTORICAL BACKGROUND

Kadıköy's old name was Chalcedon, which dates back to ancient times. Founded in the 7th century BCE by Greek settlers, Chalcedon was a hub of development for the Byzantine Empire. Over the centuries, the area has seen the Roman, Byzantine, and Ottoman rule. Today, Kadıköy is a bustling and vibrant district known for its lively atmosphere, diverse population, and thriving arts and entertainment scene. It is also a major commercial and transportation hub, hosting various businesses and cultural venues.

Üsküdar was formerly known as Skoutarion, and its history dates back to the 7th century BCE. Like Kadıköy, it became part of the Roman, Byzantine, and Ottoman empires during different periods. Üsküdar is renowned for its historic mosques, palaces, and traditional Ottoman architecture, which reflect its centuries-old heritage. The district also offers stunning views of the European side of Istanbul and the iconic landmarks that grace its skyline.

MAIN ATTRACTIONS

KADIKÖY
CULTURAL HEART AND BOHEMIAN VIBE

It wouldn't be wrong to say that Kadıköy stands as the cultural heart of Istanbul's Asian side as it's known for its bohemian atmosphere and artistic spirit. The district is a melting pot of cultures, hosting many art galleries, theaters, and music venues. This place won't disappoint you if you appreciate art from different cultures.

Although you might need to check online and reserve a spot for theater performances, film screenings, and certain events, most places in Kadıköy have opening hours between 09:00 AM to 08:00 PM. However, please make sure to double-check the opening hours online should there be any slight changes to their schedule.

Did You Know?

Kadıköy has a rich tradition of hosting independent film festivals, creating a vibrant film culture that adds to its bohemian charm.

MODA NEIGHBORHOOD

The Moda neighborhood within Kadıköy is an upscale enclave filled with trendy cafes, vintage shops, and colorful street art. It's a hub for artists, musicians, and creatives, making it a must-visit for people seeking an authentic experience.

Address: Caferaga, 34710 Kadikoy/Istanbul, Turkiye.

Did You Know?

Moda houses Istanbul's oldest and most iconic cinemas, preserving the neighborhood's cultural legacy.

BUSTLING FISH MARKET AND STREET FOOD

Kadikoy Fish Market.[36]

The Kadıköy Fish Market is a sensory delight for visitors that welcomes locals and visitors to a bustling atmosphere where everyone can savor the freshest seafood. Surrounding eateries serve mouthwatering street food and traditional Turkish dishes. Add this area to your excursions for an original taste of Istanbul's culinary scene.

As of the writing of this book, the opening hours are every day from 09:00 AM to 08:30 PM. However, please make sure to double-check the opening hours online should there be any slight changes to their schedule.

Address: Osmanaga, Gunesli Bahce Sok, 34714 Kadikoy/Istanbul, Turkiye.

Did You Know?

The fish market is a place to indulge in seafood and a hub for socializing, where locals gather for lively conversations and shared meals.

MODA SEASIDE PROMENADE AND HAYDARPAŞA TRAIN STATION

Haydarpasa Train Station.[37]

A stroll along the scenic Moda Seaside promenade and the historic Haydarpaşa Train Station are two spots you cannot miss. The mesmerizing seaside view creates a serene atmosphere, especially during early sunrise. The train station is an architectural gem dating back to 1908 and depicts the city's railway history. Entry to the train station is free, and it's open to visitors seven days a week. Still, it is currently closed for renovations and is expected to open by 2026.

Address: Rasimpasa, 34716 Kadikoy/Istanbul, Turkiye.

Did You Know?

Haydarpaşa Train Station was the main gateway for the Orient Express, connecting Istanbul to various European cities during its heyday.

ÜSKÜDAR
HISTORIC AND SPIRITUAL ÜSKÜDAR

Üsküdar is a district steeped in history and spirituality, featuring landmarks showcasing the city's rich heritage. The Şemsi Pasha Mosque is a well-preserved Ottoman architectural masterpiece and an authentic depiction of the district's cultural influence.

MAIDEN'S TOWER

Maiden's Tower.[38]

The Maiden's Tower (Kız Kulesi) is a captivating structure surrounded by legends. You can enjoy panoramic views of Istanbul and the Bosphorus while immersing yourself in the tower's intriguing tales and history.

Suppose you haven't already purchased the Museum Pass Istanbul or Turkey. In that case, the ticket to the tower costs 400TL and an additional 50 Lira for the boat ride.

As of the writing of this book, the opening hours are from 09:30 AM to 08:00 PM. However, please make sure to double-check the opening hours online should there be any slight changes to their schedule.

Address: Salacak, 34668 Uskudar/Istanbul, Turkiye.

Did You Know?

The Maiden's Tower was used for various purposes throughout history, including a lighthouse, customs station, and quarantine station during times of plague.

OTTOMAN-ERA NEIGHBORHOODS AND TEA GARDENS

Üsküdar has charming Ottoman-era neighborhoods with narrow cobblestone streets, historic houses, and vibrant tea gardens along the waterfront. These areas give you a glimpse into the district's past. Visiting these areas is a tranquil escape from the bustling city life. Çınaraltı Tea Garden is one of the most popular and is open round the clock for visitors.

Çınaraltı Tea Garden Address: Cengelkoy, Cengelkoy Mah. Cengelkoy Cad, Cinarli Cami Sk. No:4, 34680 Uskudar/Istanbul. Turkiye.

Did You Know?

Üsküdar's tea gardens have been popular meeting spots for locals for centuries, and the practice is still popular today.

SERENE AMBIANCE AND SUNSET VIEWS

Üsküdar has a tranquil ambiance, especially during the evening when the sun sets over the Bosphorus. The waterfront becomes a peaceful retreat, ideal for enjoying the beauty of the surroundings and experiencing the tranquility that Üsküdar is known for.

Did You Know?

Üsküdar is one of the best spots in Istanbul to witness stunning sunset views with a captivating backdrop to the cityscape across the water.

SPECTACULAR VIEWS OF CAMLICA HILL

Rated as the second most popular attraction in Üsküdar, Camlica Hill will captivate you with its mesmerizing views. Even though you can take a taxi to the top, an uphill walk is recommended for the full experience.

Camlica Hill Views.[39]

As of the writing of this book, the opening hours are from 10:00 AM to 09:30 PM. However, please make sure to double-check the opening hours online should there be any slight changes to their schedule.

Address: Kisikli, Camlica Tepesi yl No:25/10, 34692 Uskudar/Istanbul, Turkiye.

TRANSPORT

KADIKÖY
FERRY TERMINAL

Kadıköy is a central transportation hub with a bustling ferry terminal connecting the Asian side to various points on the European side of Istanbul. The ferry ride travels through breathtaking views of the city skyline and is an iconic way to cross the Bosphorus.

Did You Know?

The Kadıköy ferry terminal is one of the oldest and busiest in Istanbul, where you can learn more about the city's maritime history.

PUBLIC TRANSPORTATION

The district is well-connected by an extensive network of buses, dolmuş (shared taxis), and the Istanbul Metro.

Did You Know?

The historic Haydarpaşa Train Station in Kadıköy was a major railway terminal connecting Istanbul to Anatolia and beyond. Although currently closed for renovations, it remains a symbol of the city's railway heritage.

WALKING AND CYCLING

Kadıköy is a pedestrian-friendly district with well-maintained sidewalks, making it perfect for exploring on foot. The Moda neighborhood, in particular, can also be explored through leisurely strolls. Renting a bike is another way to navigate the area.

ÜSKÜDAR
FERRY SERVICES

Üsküdar is another key ferry terminal on the Asian side, offering frequent services to various destinations on the European side. The ferry is an efficient mode of transport and offers a scenic journey along the Bosphorus.

Did You Know?

During the ferry ride from Üsküdar, you will be welcomed by stunning views of Istanbul's historic skyline, including iconic landmarks like the Hagia Sophia and the Blue Mosque.

METRO AND BUSES

Üsküdar is well-connected to the broader Istanbul transport network, with metro and bus services facilitating easy travel within the district and to other parts of the city.

Did You Know?

The Marmaray is an underwater railway tunnel that connects Üsküdar to the European side of Istanbul.

TAXI AND DOLMUŞ

Taxis and dolmuş (shared taxis) are readily available in Üsküdar to get around locally.

Did You Know?

Üsküdar's waterfront is a popular spot for dolmuş rides. These rides are a memorable experience of traveling with locals while enjoying scenic views of the Bosphorus.

EXPERIENCES

KADIKÖY
STREET ART EXPLORATION IN MODA

Immerse yourself in Kadıköy's vibrant Moda neighborhood, renowned for its street art scene. Take a self-guided walking tour to discover colorful murals, graffiti, and art installations adorning the streets,

showcasing the district's bohemian spirit. You can also consider joining a guided street art tour to better connect with the local art scene and to hear the stories behind the captivating street artworks.

CULINARY ADVENTURE IN THE FISH MARKET

If you are a foodie, you don't want to miss Kadıköy's lively Fish Market. Engage your senses as you explore the stalls brimming with fresh seafood and sample delicious street food and traditional Turkish dishes.

Food tours are also available to take you through the bustling market so you can savor the best flavors while learning about the region's culinary history.

MODA SEASIDE PROMENADE SUNSET WALK

Watch the breathtaking sunset over the Marmara Sea by strolling along the Moda seaside promenade. Enjoy the gentle sea breeze, and capture stunning views of the Istanbul skyline as the sun sets.

HAYDARPAŞA TRAIN STATION TOUR

Explore the iconic Haydarpaşa Train Station, an architectural gem that reflects the grandeur of Istanbul's railway history. Although the station is currently closed for renovations, guided tours are available to take you into its rich past.

Haydarpaşa Train Station.[40]

ÜSKÜDAR
SPIRITUAL JOURNEY THROUGH OTTOMAN-ERA MOSQUES

Dive deep into Üsküdar's rich history by exploring its magnificent mosques like the Şemsi Pasha Mosque. Experience the spiritual ambiance and marvel at the intricate Ottoman architecture that graces these sacred sites. Although most mosques in Üsküdar are open 24 hours a day, some can remain closed to visitors on a local festival.

MAIDEN'S TOWER LEGENDS AND VIEWS

Discover the enchanting stories surrounding the Maiden's Tower (Kız Kulesi) and enjoy panoramic views of Istanbul and the Bosphorus. Learn about the tower's fascinating history and its role in the city's maritime past. You can take a boat tour that includes a visit to the Maiden's Tower, allowing you to appreciate both its historical significance and the stunning vistas it provides.

Maiden's Tower (Kız Kulesi).[41]

HISTORICAL NEIGHBORHOODS AND TEA GARDENS EXPLORATION

Wander through Üsküdar's charming Ottoman-era neighborhoods with narrow streets and historic houses. Stop by waterfront tea gardens to relax, enjoy traditional Turkish tea, and soak in the serene ambiance. Join a walking tour that takes you through Üsküdar's historical neighborhoods and into the district's past and present.

BOSPHORUS SUNSET CRUISE

Add a memorable experience to your Üsküdar visit by taking a Bosphorus sunset cruise. Witness the changing colors of the sky as the sun sets over the Bosphorus, casting a golden glow on Istanbul's landmarks. Sunset cruises can take you on this magical ride during the evening hours.

FAMILY FUN

KADIKÖY
KADIKÖY TOY MUSEUM

Bring the family to the Kadıköy Toy Museum. This delightful attraction showcases a vast collection of toys from different eras. It's an interactive experience where children and adults can explore the nostalgic world of toys.

Before your visit, check for special events or workshops at the museum that provide hands-on activities for kids to enjoy.

As of the writing of this book, the opening hours are Tuesday to Friday from 10 AM to 6 PM. Saturday and Sunday from 10 AM to 6:30 PM. Closed on Monday. However, please make sure to double-check the opening hours online should there be any slight changes to their schedule.

Address: Goztepe, Dr. Zeki Zeren Sk No:15, 34730 Kadikoy/Istanbul, Turkiye.

MODA SAHIL PARK

Moda Sahil Park is situated along the shoreline and is perfect for family picnics and outdoor activities. The playground is filled with engaging activities for your little ones. At the same time, the whole family can enjoy a relaxing day by the sea. Don't forget to pack a picnic basket when you visit and take in the scenic views of the Marmara Sea.

As of the writing of this book, the Moda Sahil Park is open 24 hours every day. However, please make sure to double-check the opening hours online should there be any slight changes to their schedule.

Address: Caferaga, Kucukmoda Burnu Sk No:21, 34710 Kadikoy/Istanbul, Turkiye.

TURVAK CINEMA MUSEUM

Visit the Turvak Cinema Museum in Kadıköy, which introduces you to the history of Turkish cinema. It's an engaging experience for film enthusiasts and families alike, with exhibits showcasing the evolution of cinema in Turkey. The Museum also offers interactive exhibits for kids and family-friendly screenings, but you must check the museum's schedule.

As of the writing of this book, the Turvak Cinema Museum is open Tuesday to Sunday from 10:00 AM to 6:00 PM and is closed on Monday. However, please make sure to double-check the opening hours online should there be any slight changes to their schedule.

Address: Kavacik, Sht. Tegmen Ali Yilmaz Sk. No:4, 34810 Beykoz/Istanbul, Turkiye.

KADIKÖY PUBLIC GARDEN (KADIKÖY HALK BAHÇESI)

The Kadıköy public garden in the heart of the district is a green oasis providing a space for families to unwind. With walking paths, playgrounds, and open spaces, it's an ideal spot for a family-friendly day out.

Address: Zuhtupasa, Taskopru Cd., 34724 Kadikoy/Istanbul, Turkiye.

ÜSKÜDAR
ŞEMSI PASHA MOSQUE GARDENS

Explore the gardens surrounding the Şemsi Pasha Mosque in Üsküdar to enjoy its peaceful environment. The well-maintained green spaces with a relaxing setting are perfect for a family stroll or a leisurely afternoon.

The Şemsi Pasha Mosque.[42]

Address: Mimarsinan Mh., 34664 Uskudar/Istanbul, Turkiye.

WHERE TO EAT

KADIKÖY
ÇIYA SOFRASI

Located in Kadıköy, Çiya Sofrası is well-known for its authentic Turkish cuisine. The restaurant has a diverse menu featuring traditional dishes from various regions of Turkey, taking you on a culinary journey for your taste buds.

Address: Caferaga, Gunesli Bahce Sok, 34710 Kadikoy/Istanbul, Turkiye.

ORGANIK KANTIN

For a contemporary dining experience, visit Organik Kantin in Kadıköy. This stylish restaurant is known for its modern Turkish cuisine. The menu is curated by chef Semsa Denizsel, a famous chef of Turkish origin who has been putting Turkish culinary delights on the world map.

Address: Kosuyolu, Kosuyolu Cd. No:99, 34718 Kadikoy/Istanbul, Turkiye.

HANE KADIKÖY

If you're a seafood enthusiast, Ala Kadıköy Meyhane is a must-visit. This restaurant serves fresh and delicious seafood dishes in a rustic setting. The menu features a variety of grilled fish, mezes, and traditional Turkish appetizers.

Address: Caferaga, Yasa Cd. 58/A, 34734 Kadıköy/Istanbul, Turkiye.

ÜSKÜDAR
Mado

Mado, a famous Turkish chain, is known for its delightful desserts, including ice cream and baklava.

Address: Mimar Sinan, Selmanaga Sk., 34672 Üsküdar/Istanbul, Turkiye.

KANAAT LOKANTASI

For a taste of home-cooked Turkish meals, head to Kanaat Lokantası in Üsküdar. This traditional lokanta (eatery) serves daily specials, offering a genuine Turkish dining experience focusing on local flavors.

Address: Sultantepe, Selmani Pak Cd. No:9, 34674 Üsküdar/Istanbul, Turkiye.

VILLA BOSPHORUS (BOĞAZ ET LOKANTASI)

Enjoy a captivating dining experience at Bosphorus Grill along the waterfront in Üsküdar. This restaurant specializes in Turkish grilled meats and kebabs.

Address: Beylerbeyi, Beylerbeyi Iskele cd. 18 A D:18 A, 34676 Üsküdar/Istanbul, Turkiye.

MIM KAHVE ÜSKÜDAR

Mim Kahve Üsküdar is a trendy café in Üsküdar, perfect for a casual meal or a coffee break. The menu includes a variety of sandwiches, salads, and Turkish breakfast options. The cozy atmosphere and friendly staff make it popular among locals and visitors.

Address: Sultantepe, Selmani Pak Cd. No:31 D:10, 34674 Üsküdar/Istanbul, Turkiye.

KADIKÖY AND ÜSKÜDAR (JOINT RECOMMENDATION)
Ciya Kebap

Ciya Kebap, a well-known establishment with locations in both Kadıköy and Üsküdar, is celebrated for its delicious kebabs and traditional Turkish dishes. The restaurant focuses on using high-quality ingredients and offers a diverse menu.

SHOPPING GUIDE

KADIKÖY
KADIKÖY FISH MARKET (BALIK PAZARI)

Dive into the vibrant atmosphere of Kadıköy Fish Market, where you can find an array of fresh seafood, spices, and local produce. Take home some Turkish spices or freshly caught fish for a seafood extravaganza.

Address: Osmanga, Gunesli Bahce Sok, 34714 Kadıköy/Istanbul, Turkiye.

KADIKÖY MARKET (KADIKÖY ÇARŞI)

Explore the bustling Kadıköy Market for a diverse shopping experience. This market has everything from clothing and accessories to spices and sweets. Bargaining is common here, so don't hesitate to negotiate for the best prices.

Address: Osmanga, Sogutlu Cesme Cd., 34714 Kadıköy/Istanbul, Turkiye.

MODA CADDESI

Moda Caddesi, the main street in the Moda neighborhood, is lined with boutique shops, vintage stores, and trendy cafes. Stroll along this lively avenue to discover designer fashions, eclectic accessories, and handcrafted items.

Address: Caferaga, 34710 Kadıköy/Istanbul, Turkiye.

NAUTILUS KITAP

Book lovers shouldn't miss Nautilus Kitap, a charming bookstore in Kadıköy. Browse through its collection of Turkish and international titles, including novels, art books, and unique first editions.

Address: Valide-i Atik Mahallesi Çinili Mescit Sk. Yavuz apt. 35A, Üsküdar, Turkiye.

ÜSKÜDAR
BAĞDAT CADDESI

Bağdat Caddesi, one of Istanbul's longest shopping streets, is in Üsküdar. This upscale avenue is home to international and local brands, offering a mix of fashion, accessories, and lifestyle products.

ÜSKÜDAR ANTIQUE MARKET (ANTIKA PAZARI)

Antique enthusiasts will appreciate the Üsküdar Antique Market, where you can find a curated selection of vintage items, including furniture, jewelry, and collectibles.

Address: Mimar Sinan, Kucuk Sarmasik Sokak No:1 A101 den Yukari, solda, 34672 Üsküdar/Istanbul, Turkiye.

ÜSKÜDAR HAFIZ AHMET PAŞA MARKET

For a taste of traditional Turkish bazaars, visit the Hafız Ahmet Paşa Market in Üsküdar. This market has various goods, from spices and sweets to textiles and souvenirs. It's a great place to experience the lively atmosphere of a local market.

Address: Aziz Mahmut Hudati, Uncular Cd. No:21 D:3B, 34672 Üsküdar/Istanbul, Turkiye.

AKASYA ACIBADEM SHOPPING MALL

If you prefer a modern shopping experience, head to the Akasya Acıbadem Shopping Mall in Üsküdar. This contemporary mall houses a selection of international and Turkish brands alongside restaurants, cafes, and entertainment options.

Address: Acibadem, Cecen Sok. No:25, 34660 Üsküdar/Istanbul, Turkiye.

KADIKÖY AND ÜSKÜDAR (JOINT RECOMMENDATION)

Bosphorus Cruise Souvenirs

Whether in Kadıköy or Üsküdar, take advantage of the Bosphorus cruises departing from both districts to buy unique souvenirs. Local vendors on the cruise boats also sell a variety of Turkish crafts, ceramics, and textiles, so you can shop while enjoying breathtaking views of Istanbul.

ENTERTAINMENT

KADIKÖY BARLAR SOKAĞI (BAR STREET)

Dive into Kadıköy's lively nightlife on Barlar Sokağı, a street lined with bars, pubs, and cafes. It's the perfect place to experience the district's vibrant social scene. From live music to DJ performances, you can enjoy it all in one place.

KADIKÖY HAYAL KAHVESI

Music enthusiasts should check out Kadıköy Hayal Kahvesi, a popular venue for live performances. From rock and jazz to Turkish pop, this venue hosts a variety of concerts, creating a dynamic and energetic atmosphere. Keep an eye on the schedule for upcoming concerts and events, and book tickets in advance for a night of memorable live music.

Address: Caferaga Mh., Rihtim Sk., 34710 Kadıköy/Istanbul, Turkiye.

KADIKÖY BULL STATUE (BOĞA HEYKELI)

The Kadıköy Bull Statue, a district symbol, is a cultural landmark and a gathering spot for street musicians

and performers. You can spend time people-watching around the Bull Statue and get lost in spontaneous artistic expression.

The Kadıköy Bull Statue.[43]

Address: Altiyol Meydai, Sogutlu Cesme Cd, 34714 Kadıköy/Istanbul, Turkiye.

ÜSKÜDAR
ÜSKÜDAR MIHRIMAH SULTAN SAHNESI

Theater enthusiasts can visit Üsküdar Mihrimah Sultan Sahnesi, a cultural venue hosting performances, including plays, concerts, and dance shows. If you are interested, check the schedule for upcoming performances and cultural events.

ÇAMLICA HILL (ÇAMLICA TEPESI)

While Çamlıca Hill is primarily known for its panoramic views, it also has entertainment options like cafes and restaurants where you can enjoy a meal while taking in the breathtaking scenery.

ACCOMMODATIONS

KADIKÖY
DOUBLETREE BY HILTON ISTANBUL MODA

DoubleTree by Hilton Istanbul Moda welcomes guests with contemporary rooms, a rooftop pool with breathtaking views, and convenient access to Moda's vibrant neighborhood. The hotel is a perfect blend of comfort and sophistication.

Address: Caferaga, Albay Falk Sozdener Cd. No:3, 34710 Kadıköy/ Istanbul, Turkiye.

ÜSKÜDAR
SWISSOTEL THE BOSPHORUS ISTANBUL

Swissotel The Bosphorus Istanbul is a short distance from Üsküdar. It's a five-star hotel with luxurious rooms, multiple dining options, and spa facilities. Situated along the Bosphorus, it provides stunning views of the strait and the city.

Address: Visnezade, Acisu Sokagi No:19, 34357 Üsküdar/Istanbul, Turkiye.

ELITE MARMARA BOSPHORUS & OTEL CAMLICA

Elite Marmara Bosphorus & Otel Camlica is a beautiful hotel. Featuring elegant rooms, a beautiful garden, and a range of dining choices, this is a luxury experience worth every cent.

Address: Kucuk Camlica, Sht. Serhat Emre Sk. No:27, 34000 Üsküdar/Istanbul, Turkiye.

SUMAHAN ON THE WATER

Located in the Asian side of Istanbul, Sumahan on the Water offers a boutique hotel experience with stylish rooms and a mesmerizing view of the landscape of the Bosphorus. This waterfront hotel is a tranquil escape while still being accessible to both Kadıköy and Üsküdar.

Address: Cengelkoy, Kuleli Cd. No:43, 34684 Üsküdar/Istanbul, Turkiye.

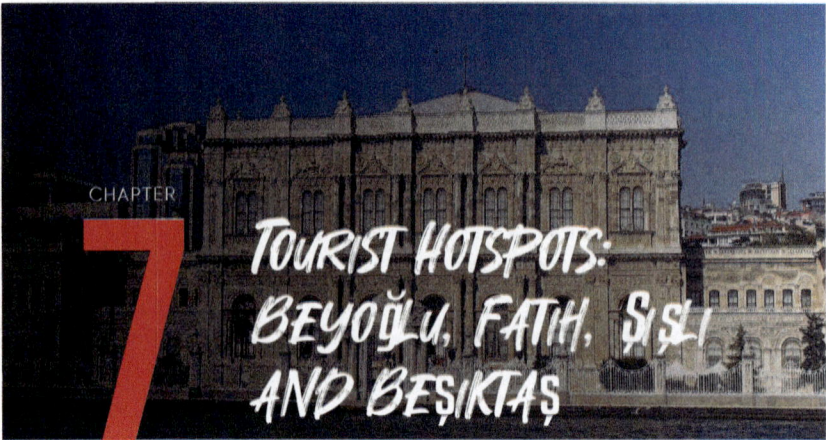

7
TOURIST HOTSPOTS: BEYOĞLU, FATIH, ŞIŞLI AND BEŞIKTAŞ

The districts of Beyoğlu, Fatih, Şişli, and Beşiktaş are some enticing tourist hotspots of Istanbul, Turkey. Situated on the European side of the city, each district has its own vibe. From the bustling streets of Beyoğlu to the ancient landmarks of Fatih, the cosmopolitan ambiance of Şişli, and the waterfront allure of Beşiktaş, these areas reflect Istanbul's diverse cultural and historical heritage.

Beyoğlu, Fatih, Şişli, and Beşiktaş on the map.[44]

HISTORICAL BACKGROUND

BEYOĞLU

Historically known as Pera, Beyoğlu has been a focal point of cultural exchange and cosmopolitan life. During the 19th and 20th centuries, it flourished as a center for foreign embassies and cultural institutions, shaping its modern identity as a dynamic hub for entertainment, commerce, and art.

FATIH

Formerly Constantinople, Fatih is Istanbul's historical heart. Its iconic landmarks, including the Hagia Sophia and Topkapi Palace, bear witness to centuries of Byzantine and Ottoman history, making it a melting pot of cultural and religious heritage.

ŞİŞLİ

Once a quiet residential area, Şişli underwent rapid urbanization in the late 19th and early 20th centuries. It's a modern district with commercial centers, upscale neighborhoods, and cultural venues, reflecting the city's evolution.

BEŞİKTAŞ

With a name derived from the Turkish word beşik (cradle), Beşiktaş was the hub of maritime activities during the Ottoman era. The district blends historic charm with a lively atmosphere, featuring the iconic Dolmabahçe Palace and various popular destinations for visitors.

MAIN ATTRACTIONS

BEYOĞLU

Beyoğlu is Istanbul's cultural and artistic heartbeat. It's a district that pulsates with vibrant energy and has evolved into a dynamic hub where tradition meets modernity.

Istiklal Street: You will be star-struck by the lively ambiance of Istiklal Street. It's a bustling pedestrian avenue with shops, cafes, and historical landmarks like the Çiçek Pasajı (Flower Passage), Roman Catholic churches of Santa Maria Draperis, the Balık Pazarı (The Fish Market), and the list goes on. It's a journey through time and culture, where the past seamlessly blends with contemporary flair.

Istiklal Street.[45]

Galata Tower: Rise above the city at the iconic Galata Tower, which offers panoramic views of Istanbul. This medieval stone tower symbolizes Beyoğlu's enduring charm. It is a not-to-miss spot in your attractions-to-visit checklist.

Galata Tower.[46]

As of the writing of this book, the Galata Tower is open every day from 08:30 AM to 10:00 PM. However, please make sure to double-check the opening hours online should there be any slight changes to their schedule.

Address: Bereketzade, 34421 Beyoğlu/Istanbul, Turkiye.

Pera Museum: Explore the Pera Museum, a cultural gem with a notable art collection, including Anatolian weights and measures, Orientalist paintings, and works by renowned Turkish artists. The museum truly exhibits Beyoğlu's commitment to the arts.

Pera Museum.[47]

As of the writing of this book, the Pera Museum is open Tuesday to Sunday from 10:00 AM to 07:00 PM and is closed on Monday. However, please make sure to double-check the opening hours online should there be any slight changes to their schedule.

Address: Asmali Mescit, Mesrutiyet Cd. No:65, 34430 Beyoğlu/Istanbul, Turkiye.

Did You Know?

Istiklal Street was once the main avenue for the city's foreign residents during the Ottoman era, reflecting the multicultural history that shaped Beyoğlu's cosmopolitan identity.

BEŞIKTAŞ

Beşiktaş is a lively district on the European side where the football culture thrives. The district is home to a renowned football club in Turkey, where you will witness historical charm combined seamlessly with a modern, energetic atmosphere.

Dolmabahçe Palace: Immerse yourself in the luxury of Dolmabahçe Palace, a grandeur symbol of Ottoman architecture and the administrative center during the late empire.

Dolmabahçe Palace.[48]

As of the writing of this book, the opening hours are Tuesday to Sunday from 09:00 AM to 05:30 PM and closed Monday. However, please make sure to double-check the opening hours online should there be any slight changes to their schedule.

Address: Visnezade, Dolmabahçe Cd., 34357 Beşiktaş/Istanbul, Turkiye.

Fish Market and Bosphorus Ferry Ride: Don't forget to visit the lively fish market, indulging yourself in the local culinary scene. To enjoy the coastal beauty of Beşiktaş, a Bosphorus ferry ride is also available for visitors.

As of the writing of this book, the Fish Market is open every day from 10:30 AM to 09:15 PM. However, please make sure to double-check the opening hours online should there be any slight changes to their schedule.

Fish Market Address: Sinanpasa, Koyici Cd No:19, 34353 Beşiktaş/Istanbul, Turkiye.

You can also take a cruise and see things from a different perspective:

- **All-Day Cruise**: *Starts at 09:00 AM*

- **Morning Sightseeing Cruise**: *Starts by 10:00 AM*

- **Evening Sightseeing Cruise**: *Starts by 06:00 PM*

- **Bosphorus Lunch Cruises**: *12:30 PM to 05:00 PM*

The district has a youthful vibe featuring student-filled cafes and lively bars, especially around the vibrant Beşiktaş Square, where locals gather especially to celebrate their team's victories.

Did You Know?

Beşiktaş has a particular connection to sea travel as its name translates to "Cradle Stone." It is believed to reference the ancient rocks used to secure ships in the area.

FATIH

Fatih is the historical core of Istanbul, where you can immerse yourself in the city's Byzantine and Ottoman heritage. This district resonates with an ancient charm, echoing tales of empires and cultural richness.

Grand Bazaar and Suleymaniye Mosque: Explore the labyrinthine alleys of the Grand Bazaar, a historic marketplace offering a vibrant array of goods. Another nearby place to visit is the awe-inspiring Suleymaniye Mosque. It's a masterpiece of Ottoman architecture.

Grand Bazaar Istanbul.[49]

As of the writing of this book, the Grand Bazaar is open from 09:00 AM to 07:00 PM every day except for Sundays. However, please make sure to double-check the opening hours online should there be any slight changes to their schedule.

As of the writing of this book, the Suletmaniye Mosque is open every day from 08:30 AM to 04:45 PM. However, please make sure to double-check the opening hours online should there be any slight changes to their schedule.

Grand Bazaar Address: Beyazit, 34126 Fatih/Istanbul, Turkiye.

Suleymaniye Mosque Address: Suleymaniye, Prof. Siddik Sami Onar Cd. No:1, 34116 Fatih/Istanbul, Turkiye.

Chora Church: Discover the lesser-known gem of Fatih, the Chora Church, which preserves exquisite mosaics illustrating biblical scenes. It's a hidden treasure reflecting the district's rich artistic legacy, even under different rules.

Chora Church.[50]

As of the writing of this book, the Chora Church is open every day from 09:00 AM to 06:30 PM. However, please make sure to double-check the opening hours online should there be any slight changes to their schedule.

Address: Dervis Ali, Kariye Cami Sk. No:18, 34087 Fatih/Istanbul, Turkiye.

Traditional Eateries: You don't want to miss the rich flavors of traditional Turkish dishes at authentic eateries scattered throughout Fatih.

Did You Know?

The Grand Bazaar is one of the world's oldest and largest covered markets, dating back to the 15th century.

ŞİŞLİ

Şişli is a modern commercial and residential district with shopping centers, cultural sites, and architectural gems.

Cevahir Mall: Dive into retail therapy at Cevahir Mall. It's one of the largest shopping centers in Europe, with stores stocking many international and local brands.

Cevahir Mall.[51]

As of the writing of this book, the Cevahir Mall is open every day from 10:00 AM to 10:00 PM. However, please make sure to double-check the opening hours online should there be any slight changes to their schedule.

Address: 19 Mayis, Buyukdere Cd. No:22, 34360 Şişli/Istanbul, Turkiye.

Atatürk Museum and Maçka Park: Visit the Atatürk Museum to learn about the founder of modern Turkey or the Maçka Park oasis for a tranquil visit within the urban landscape.

Maçka Park.[52]

As of the writing of this book, the Atatürk Museum is open every day from 10:00 AM to 05:00 PM. However, please make sure to double-check the opening hours online should there be any slight changes to their schedule.

As of the writing of this book, the Maçka Park is open 24 hours every day. However, please make sure to double-check the opening hours online should there be any slight changes to their schedule.

Atatürk Museum Address: Mesrutiyet, Halaskargazi Cd. No:140, 34363 Şişli/Istanbul, Turkiye.

Maçka Park Address: Harbiye, Macka Cd., 34000 Şişli/Istanbul, Turkiye.

Nişantaşı: Explore Nişantaşı within Şişli, known for luxury shopping and trendy cafes, blending modern architecture with a sophisticated ambiance.

Ihlamur Palace: Now a public museum, it was originally an imperial Ottoman Palace surrounded by linden trees. The establishment houses two mansions, each a fine example of a blend of Western and Turkish architectural characteristics. It was constructed in the period of Sultan Abdülmecid I, so it is the perfect place to discover the history and learn about the architecture of the

time. A pleasant stroll in the gardens and a cup of Turkish coffee within the palace brings a day of fascination to a perfect end.

Ihlamur Palace.[53]

As of the writing of this book, the opening hours are every day from 09:00 AM to 05:00 PM. However, please make sure to double-check the opening hours online should there be any slight changes to their schedule.

Address: Tesvikiye, Nisantasi Ihlamur Yolu Sk., 34357 Şişli/Istanbul, Turkiye.

Did You Know?

Şişli's architectural landscape features a striking mix of Art Nouveau buildings from the early 20th century and sleek modern skyscrapers, symbolizing the district's evolution from a residential area to a dynamic commercial center.

TRANSPORT

BEYOĞLU

+ **Public Transport**: *Beyoğlu has various transportation options, including buses, trams, and the iconic Istanbul Metro. The Tünel, one of the world's oldest subways, connects Karaköy to Beyoğlu.*

+ **Istiklal Street Nostalgic Tram**: *Take your commuting experience up a notch by riding on a nostalgic tram along Istiklal Street.*

+ **Beşiktaş**

+ **Bosphorus Ferry**: *It's an easy and scenic way to travel the European and Asian sides of Istanbul while enjoying breathtaking cityscape views. You can find the ferry from Beşiktaş.*

+ **Public Transportation Hub**: *As a transportation hub, Beşiktaş is well-connected with buses, dolmuş (shared taxis), and taxis for seamless travel anywhere.*

FATIH

+ **Tram and Metro**: *Fatih is well-connected through tram lines, giving access to major attractions like the Grand Bazaar and Sultanahmet Square. The metro system also connects the district to various parts of Istanbul.*

+ **Walking Exploration**: *Given the area's historical density, exploring Fatih on foot is a rewarding experience. Many attractions are within walking distance of each other.*

ŞİŞLİ

+ **Metro and Bus Networks**: *Şişli also has a well-developed metro network, including the M2 and M6 lines, making it easy to navigate the district and connect to other parts of Istanbul. Numerous bus routes are also available.*

+ **Taxis and Rideshare**: *Taxis and rideshare services are readily available in Şişli for those who prefer a more direct and personalized mode of transportation.*

+ **General Tips**

+ *Consider obtaining an Istanbulkart, a rechargeable smart card that provides access to public transportation at discounted rates and is a convenient way to travel.*

- *Istanbul is known for its traffic, especially during peak hours. Plan your journeys accordingly, and be aware that some areas may be more accessible by foot or public transport.*

EXPERIENCES

BEYOĞLU

Artistic Exploration: Dive into Beyoğlu's creative heart by exploring galleries along Istiklal Street, like the Pera Museum. Attend live performances at venues like Babylon or enjoy a film at the historic Atlas Cinema for a taste of Istanbul's vibrant cultural scene.

Nightlife Tour: You can also take a night tour along Istiklal Street, discovering rooftop bars with panoramic views, live music venues, and traditional meyhanes (traditional Turkish bars). The district's nightlife comes alive after sunset, offering an unforgettable experience.

BEŞIKTAŞ

Football Match Experience: Immerse yourself in Beşiktaş's passionate football culture by attending a match at the Vodafone Park Stadium. The electric atmosphere and cheering fans create a unique sporting experience. However,

before visiting, do check for the schedule and entry tickets.

Bosphorus Cruise: Take a Bosphorus cruise departing from Beşiktaş for spectacular views of Istanbul's landmarks, including the Dolmabahçe Palace and the historic waterfront. Sunset cruises add a romantic touch if you are traveling with a partner.

FATIH

Historical Walking Tour: Take a walking tour through Fatih, exploring iconic sites like the Grand Bazaar, Suleymaniye Mosque, and Chora Church. Guided tours are also available if you want to learn about the district's rich Byzantine and Ottoman heritage.

Culinary Adventure: Indulge in a culinary adventure in Fatih, sampling traditional Turkish dishes at local eateries and street food stalls within the Grand Bazaar.

ŞIŞLI

Luxury Shopping in Nişantaşı: Experience the chic side of Şişli by visiting Nişantaşı, renowned for its luxury boutiques and trendy cafes. Stroll, shop for designer items, and savor Turkish coffee in this upscale district.

Art and History at Atatürk Museum: Visit the Atatürk Museum in Şişli to learn about the founder of modern Turkey. The museum showcases personal belongings and historical artifacts from Atatürk's life.

THEMATIC SIGHTSEEING TIPS

Guided Tours: Consider joining guided thematic tours like the street art walks in Beyoğlu, historical storytelling in Fatih, football culture tours in Beşiktaş, and architectural tours highlighting Şişli's diverse structures.

Festivals and Events: Always check the local event calendar for festivals and events in these districts. For example, Beyoğlu hosts the Istanbul International Film Festival, while Beşiktaş often hosts cultural and music events.

FAMILY FUN

BEYOĞLU

Istiklal Street Stroll: Istiklal Street is family-friendly, where you can explore a variety of shops, indulge in street food, and encounter street performers to enjoy the lively atmosphere.

BEŞIKTAŞ

Dolmabahçe Palace Gardens: While the Dolmabahçe Palace itself may not be ideal for energetic youngsters, the expansive gardens are a perfect setting for a relaxing family picnic.

Bosphorus Ferry Adventure: Children will love a Bosphorus ferry ride where they can spot seagulls and enjoy the sea breeze.

FATIH

Miniaturk: Explore Miniaturk is a miniature park featuring scaled-down replicas of famous landmarks from Turkey and around the world. It's an educational and entertaining experience for both children and adults.

As of the writing of this book, the opening hours are every day from 09:00 AM to 06:00 PM. However, please make sure to double-check the opening hours online should there be any slight changes to their schedule.

Address: Ornektepe, Imrahor Cd. No:7, 34445 Beyoglu/Istanbul, Turkiye.

ŞIŞLI

Cevahir Mall Entertainment: Cevahir Mall in Şişli offers shopping and family entertainment options,

including a cinema and an indoor amusement center, making it a one-stop destination for family fun.

WHERE TO EAT

BEYOĞLU

360 Istanbul: Perched at the top of a historical building, 360 Istanbul is where you can enjoy panoramic city views while savoring wholesome food. The restaurant serves Turkish and international cuisine, making it an ideal spot for an exceptional dining experience.

Address: Tomtom Mah. Istiklal Cad. No:163 K: 8, 34433 Beyoğlu/Istanbul, Turkiye.

Karaköy Lokantası: For a taste of Turkish home cooking with a modern twist, Karaköy Lokantası is a popular choice. The menu features a variety of mezes, kebabs, and traditional dishes in a cozy setting.

Address: Kemankes Mahallesi, Kemankes Cd. No:57, 34425 Beyoğlu/Istanbul, Turkiye.

Mikla: Located on the top floor of the Marmara Pera Hotel, Mikla combines Turkish and Scandinavian flavors.

Address: Asmali Mescit, The Marmara Pera, Mesrutiyet Cd. No: 15, 34430 Beyoğlu/Istanbul, Turkiye.

BEŞIKTAŞ

Bebek Balıkçı: Enjoy seafood with a Bosphorus view at Bebek Balıkçı. This restaurant in Beşiktaş offers a relaxed setting, ideal for families and seafood enthusiasts.

Address: Bebek, Cevdet Pasa Cd. 36/A, 34342 Beşiktaş/Istanbul, Turkiye.

Alacati Mezze House: A popular choice for grilled meats and mezes, Alacati Mezze House has a relaxing atmosphere and Turkish flavors, focusing on quality local ingredients.

Address: Akat, Haydar Aliyev Cd. No:1E, 34355 Beşiktaş/Istanbul, Turkiye.

Vogue Restaurant and Bar: This restaurant is in a historical building and serves Ottoman-inspired dishes. With a terrace overlooking the Bosphorus, it's a delightful spot for global dishes and a mesmerizing view.

Address: Visnezade, BJK Plaza, Suleyman Seba Cd. No:48, 34357 Beşiktaş/Istanbul, Turkiye.

FATIH

Asitane Restaurant: Located near the Chora Church, Asitane specializes in recreating recipes from the Ottoman palace kitchens. It's

a unique culinary experience for those interested in historical Turkish cuisine.

Address: Dervis Ali, Kariye Cami Sk. No:6, 34240 Fatih/Istanbul, Turkiye.

Fuego by Colin: For a blend of Turkish and Latin American flavors, Fuego by Colin offers a diverse menu in a stylish setting. The restaurant is known for its creative dishes and vibrant atmosphere.

Address: Alemdar Mah. Incili Cavus Sok. No:/A, 34110 Fatih/Istanbul, Turkiye.

ŞİŞLİ

Nusr-Et Steakhouse: Owned by the famous Turkish chef Nusret Gökçe, also known as Salt Bae, Nusr-Et Steakhouse in Nişantaşı is a carnivore's delight. Succulent steaks and other meat dishes are served with a theatrical flourish.

Address: Harboye, Macka Palas, Macka Cd. No:33/B, 34367 Şişli/Istanbul, Turkiye.

Delicatessen: This trendy spot in Nişantaşı offers a fusion of international flavors. It is famous for its medley of dishes and healthy menu, which includes breakfast options, burgers, and salads.

Address: Halaskargazi, Zaker Sokagi 30/A, 34371 Şişli/Istanbul, Turkiye.

Street Foods: Don't miss out on the diverse street food options, especially along Istiklal Street in Beyoğlu and around the Grand Bazaar in Fatih. Try simit (Turkish bagel), kebabs, and traditional desserts.

Tea Houses and Cafes: For a more laid-back experience, explore local tea houses (çay evi) and cafes in these districts.

SHOPPING GUIDE

BEYOĞLU

Istiklal Street: Shopaholics will find paradise on Istiklal Street, a bustling avenue filled with international and local brands, boutiques, and department stores. Explore vintage shops, trendy boutiques, and flagship stores along this iconic shopping street.

Galata Antique Bazaar: For unique and antique finds, visit the Galata Antique Bazaar. This hidden gem offers a variety of vintage items, including jewelry, furniture, and collectibles.

BEŞIKTAŞ

Nişantaşı: Known as Istanbul's luxury shopping district, Nişantaşı in Beşiktaş features high-end fashion brands, designer boutiques, and upscale department stores. It's the perfect destination for those seeking sophisticated fashion and lifestyle items.

Bebek Art Street: Bebek, a neighborhood within Beşiktaş, is home to Art Street, where you'll find art galleries, concept stores, and trendy boutiques. Explore this area for unique art pieces and stylish hand-crafted finds.

FATIH

Grand Bazaar: No shopping guide in Fatih is complete without mentioning the Grand Bazaar, one of the world's largest and oldest covered markets. With over 4,000 shops, it's a labyrinth of treasures, including jewelry, textiles, ceramics, and spices.

Spice Bazaar: Adjacent to the Grand Bazaar, the Spice Bazaar is a sensory delight. Explore stalls selling spices, teas, Turkish Delight, and other culinary specialties.

ŞIŞLI

Cevahir Mall: As one of the largest shopping malls in Europe, Cevahir Mall houses a combination of international and Turkish brands, a cinema complex, and a variety of dining options. It's a one-stop destination for fashion, electronics, and entertainment.

Nişantaşı Streets: Beyond the mall, the streets of Nişantaşı in Şişli are lined with chic boutiques, luxury brands, and trendy cafes. Explore Abdi İpekçi Street and Teşvikiye Avenue for upscale shopping experiences.

SHOPPING TIPS

✦ *In traditional markets like the Grand Bazaar, bargaining is expected. Don't hesitate to negotiate prices, but do so respectfully.*

✦ *Seek out shops that support local artisans and designers. Many districts, especially Beyoğlu and Beşiktaş, feature independent stores promoting unique, handmade products.*

ENTERTAINMENT

BEYOĞLU

Live Music at Babylon: Experience the vibrant music scene of Istanbul by attending a live performance at Babylon.

Pera Film: Film enthusiasts can explore Pera Museum's film program at Pera Film. The museum often screens independent and classic films.

BEŞIKTAŞ

Vodafone Park Events: Check the event schedule at Vodafone Park, Beşiktaş's football stadium. In addition to football matches, the stadium hosts concerts and events.

Address: Visnezade, Dolmabahce Cd. No:1 34357 Besiktas/Istanbul, Turkiye.

Cultural Performances at Akaretler Sıraevler: Akaretler Sıraevler, a historic row of buildings in Beşiktaş, occasionally hosts cultural events and performances. Keep an eye out for what is happening in this charming neighborhood.

Address: Sinanpasa Sair Nedim Cd. No:22, 34000 Beskitas/Istanbul, Turkiye.

FATIH

Whirling Dervish Performances: Witness the mesmerizing whirling dervishes in a spiritual performance. Several venues in Fatih, including the Hodjapasha Cultural Center, offer traditional Sufi music and dance shows.

Turkish Night Dinner Shows: Enjoy an evening of entertainment and traditional Turkish cuisine with dinner shows in Fatih. These shows typically include folk dances, live music, and belly dancing performances.

ŞIŞLI

Istanbul Sapphire Observation Deck: For a unique entertainment experience, visit the Istanbul Sapphire skyscraper in Şişli. The observation deck provides breathtaking views of the city.

Address: Emniyet Evleri, eski Buyukdere Cd. No:1, 34415 Sisli/Istanbul, Turkiye.

ACCOMMODATIONS

BEYOĞLU

Pera Palace Hotel: A historic landmark, the Pera Palace Hotel in Beyoğlu has hosted famous guests since its opening in 1895. With its stunning interiors, this luxurious

hotel offers a blend of history and modern comfort.

Address: Evliya Celebi, Mesrutiyet Caddesi, Tepebasi Cd. No:52, 34430 Beyoğlu/Istanbul, Turkiye.

The Marmara Pera: Located near Istiklal Street, The Marmara Pera provides contemporary accommodations with panoramic city views. The rooftop terrace offers a perfect spot to unwind and enjoy the skyline.

Address: Asmali Mescit, Mesrutiyet Cd. No:15, 34430 Beyoğlu/Istanbul, Turkiye.

BEŞIKTAŞ

Shangri-La Bosphorus: Overlooking the Bosphorus, Shangri-La Bosphorus in Beşiktaş offers opulent rooms and suites. Its spa, outdoor pool, and multiple dining options provide a luxurious retreat.

Address: Sinanpasa, Hayrettin Iskelesi Sk. D:No. 1, 34353 Beşiktaş/Istanbul, Turkiye.

FATIH

Four Seasons Hotel Istanbul at Sultanahmet: This luxurious hotel in Fatih is a converted neoclassical prison. The Four Seasons offers a serene oasis with stunning views of Hagia Sophia and the Blue Mosque.

Address: Sultanahmet, Tevkifhane Sk. No:1, 34122, Turkiye.

Hotel Sultania: Located near the Grand Bazaar, Hotel Sultania has elegant and comfortable rooms. The hotel's Ottoman-inspired decor and spa facilities make your stay in Fatih relaxing.

Address: Hoca Pasa, Mehmet Murat Sk. No 4, 34110 Fatih/Istanbul, Turkiye.

ŞIŞLI

The Ritz-Carlton, Istanbul: The Ritz-Carlton, Istanbul, offers luxurious accommodations with Bosphorus views. The hotel features an impressive spa, fine dining options, and spacious rooms for a lavish stay.

Address: Suzer Plaza Askerocagi Caddessi, Elmadag Cd. No:6, 34367 Şişli/Istanbul, Turkiye.

Park Bosphorus Hotel Istanbul: Situated in Nişantaşı, Park Bosphorus Hotel blends modernity and tradition. Its central location makes it convenient for both shopping and exploring Şişli.

Address: Tahsildar Sokak No:13/b, 34134 Fatih/Istanbul, Turkiye.

ACCOMMODATION TIPS

✦ **Boutique Hotels**: *Explore boutique hotels in Beyoğlu and Beşiktaş for unique, personalized experiences with distinctive designs and atmospheres.*

✦ **Historical Accommodations**: *In Fatih, consider staying in hotels with historical significance, providing an immersive experience within Istanbul's rich heritage.*

✦ **Business and Luxury Hotels**: *In Şişli, many accommodations cater to business travelers and those seeking upscale amenities. Look for hotels with spa facilities and rooftop views for added luxury.*

These districts offer a range of accommodations, from historic hotels to modern luxury establishments. Whether you prefer a boutique hotel in Beyoğlu or a spa retreat in Şişli, Istanbul's neighborhoods have options for every traveler's needs.

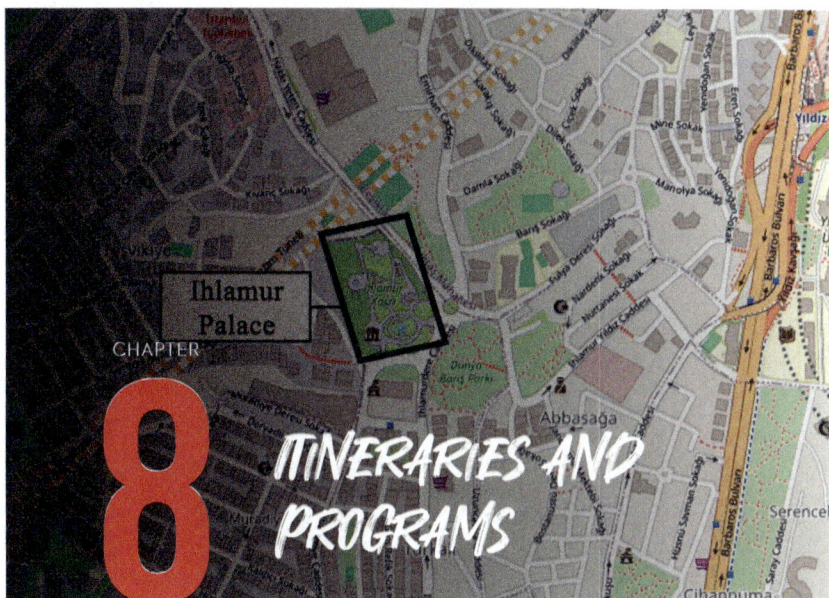

Ihlamur
Palace

CHAPTER

8 ITINERARIES AND PROGRAMS

Istanbul has so many sights to see that it's challenging to plan a comprehensive trip. With over 39 districts to explore, even a month may not be enough to visit every beautiful spot in the city. Should you explore the Asian side or the European side first? Some tourist hotspots, like Beşiktaş, may take several days to tour. What about the Princes Islands or the other lesser-known yet equally mesmerizing neighborhoods? It's better to go with experience during times like these than plan a trip from scratch. Here are a few tried and tested itineraries that have provided blissful and wholesome experiences to many travelers over the years.

Explore Istanbul in 5 days.[54]

No matter how long you stay in Istanbul, you can never really explore every nook and cranny of the place. Months (maybe even years) may be required for the task. This five-day itinerary includes as much of this fabulous city as possible without tiring you out too much.

DAY 1: TRAVELING BACK IN TIME

Day 1.[55]

✦ **Morning**: *Begin your day with a traditional Turkish breakfast at any of the eateries in Sultanahmet. Proceed to immerse yourself in Istanbul's history at the Archaeological Museum in the neighborhood. Walk to the Hagia Irene church and museum nearby to explore its history dating back to the Roman Emperor Constantine I.*

Hagia Irene Church and Museum is a 300 m walk away from the Archaeological Museum.

Istanbul Archaeological
Museum QR Code.

Hagia Irene Church and
Museum QR Code.

+ **Afternoon**: *Head back to Gulhane Park for lunch at Café Gulhane. Walk the length of the Basilica Cistern as you digest your delicious meal. Admire the Milion stone on your way to Little Hagia Sophia. Then, head to the Blue Mosque before proceeding to the main attraction, the Hagia Sophia.*

Walk 850 m from Hagia Irene Church and Museum to Gulhane Park. Basilica Cistern is a 750 m walk from Gulhane Park, and Little Hagia Sophia is a 1 km walk from the Basilica Cistern. From the Little Hagia Sophia, walk 500 m to get to the Blue Mosque. Walk 290 m from the Blue Mosque to get to the Hagia Sophia.

Address: Cankurtaran, Soğuk Çeşme Sk. No:30/B, 34122 Fatih/İstanbul, Türkiye

Gulhane Park QR Code.

Basilica Cistern QR Code.

Little Hagia Sophia QR Code.

Blue Mosque QR Code.

Hagia Sophia QR Code.

+ **Evening**: *Note that the mosque is open only until 6:30 pm. If you have taken an extended lunch, skip Basilica Cistern (open until 10:00 pm) and head directly to Hagia Sophia. Explore the cistern in the evening. End your first day with a drink near your accommodation.*

DAY 2: FAST-FORWARD TO THE PRESENT

Day 2.[56]

+ **Morning**: *Walk down the most famous avenues in the city, Istiklal Caddesi, and have breakfast at one of the quaint little cafés there. Head to Taksim Square followed by the Pera Museum of Modern Art. Proceed to admire the historical Beyoğlu and a few other galleries in the neighborhood.*

To get to Taksim Square from Istiklal Caddesi, walk 32 m to the Galatasaray Lisesi tram stop and take T2 (Taksim Meydan) to Taksim Meydan and walk 140 m. To get to the Pera Museum of Modern Art from Taksim Square, walk 100 m to the Taksim Tunel metro stop and take metro 50N (Alibeykoy Metro) to Tepebasi, then walk 500 m.

| Istiklal Caddesi QR Code. | Taksim Square QR Code. | Pera Museum of Modern Art QR Code |

+ **Afternoon**: *Have lunch at Hamdi's across the Galata Bridge. Soak in the intoxicating smells of the Spice Market. Book a ferry from Eminönü to Kadıköy on the Asian side and explore the food market. Dine at the Ciya Sofrasi restaurant to end your day.*

Day 3.[57]

+ **Morning**: *Have brunch before heading to Ortaköy mosque. The Dolmabahçe Palace, a 30-minute walk from the mosque, provides excellent insight into the history and culture of Istanbul.*

If you do not feel like walking, you can walk 260 m from Ortakoy Mosque to Orakoy-Kabatas Erkek Lisesi tram stop and take tram DT2 (Vadi) to Beskitas Stadyumu, then walk 550 m to Dolmabahce Palace.

Ortakoy Mosque QR Code.

Dolmabahce Palace QR Code.

+ **Afternoon**: *A café on the palace premises serves delectable cuisine, is perfect for lunch, and has a mesmerizing view of the Bosphorus. Then, enjoy a short walk from the Kabataş neighborhood to the Galata Mevlevi museum. The queues for the Galata Tower will take up much of your afternoon, but the views from the top are breathtaking.*

To get to the Galata Mevlevi museum from the Kabataş neighborhood, walk 550 m west on Nuri Ziya Sok.

Galata Mevlevi Museum QR Code.

Galata Tower QR Code.

+ **Evening**: *Explore a bit more of İstiklal Caddesi again and dine at Divan Brasserie Beyoglu.*

DAY 4: THE OTTOMAN AND ROMAN TOUR

Day 4.[58]

✦ **Morning**: *Break your fast at one of the restaurants near Topkapı Metro Station, and go to the Panorama 1453 History Museum, which highlights the Ottoman and Roman battles. Take the tram to Edirnekapi and explore the Kariye Mosque. From Ayvansary, take the ferry down the Bosphorus to Karaköy.*

To take the tram, walk 130 m from the Panorama 1453 History Museum to the Topkapi Panorama 1453 bus stop and take bus A27-Pazarici-Topkapi (Pazarici) to Edrinekapi, then walk 500 m to the Kariye Mosque.

Panorama 1453 History Museum QR Code

Kariye Mosque QR Code.

✦ **Afternoon**: *Before admiring Karaköy's famous art galleries, enjoy seafood cuisine at Akin Balik, which is a few blocks from the bridge.*

✦ **Evening**: *The art galleries will take all afternoon to explore. Dine at any of the restaurants in the area when the sun sets.*

Day 5.[59]

✦ **Morning**: *Have breakfast anywhere, but don't wash it down with tea or coffee yet. Head to Valens Aqueduct and down to Süleymaniye Mosque. Down the hill on the other side, you will find Aga Kapisi restaurant with superb city views from its rooftop. Have tea or coffee there.*

Walk 800 m from Valens Aqueduct to get to the Suleymaniye Mosque. Aga Kapisi restaurant is 200 m from the Suleymaniye Mosque.

Address: Süleymaniye Mah Fetva Yokuşu, Nazır İzzet Efendi Sk. No:11, 34134 Fatih/İstanbul, Türkiye

Valens Aqueduct QR Code.

Suleymaniye Mosque QR Code.

✦ **Afternoon**: *Shop for an hour or so at the Grand Bazaar and have lunch at one of the many kebab stalls there.*

Walk 750 m from Aga Kapisi restaurant to get to the Grand Bazaar.

Grand Bazaar QR Code.

✦ **Evening**: *End your final day by exploring the grand Ottoman Empire at the Topkapı Palace. Just be sure to get there before 5 PM as the palace does not let any more visitors in after this time.*

To get to Topkapi Palace, walk 120 m from the Grand Bazaar to the Beyazit-Kapalicarsi tram stop and take tram T1 (Eminonu) to Gulhane then walk 650 m.

Topkopi Palace QR Code.

4-DAY PROGRAM FOR EXPLORING BEŞIKTAŞ

Explore Beşiktaş in four days.[60]

Beşiktaş houses several of Istanbul's prominent sights, which you can explore if you have around four days to spare.

Day 1.[61]

+ **Morning**: *Start your day with a traditional Turkish breakfast at one of Beşiktaş's cozy cafés.*

+ **Afternoon**: *Visit the Dolmabahçe Palace, admiring its opulent interiors and lush gardens.*

+ **Evening**: *Stroll along the Beşiktaş waterfront and enjoy a dinner with a view of the Bosphorus.*

Day 2.[62]

✦ **Morning**: *Explore the Naval Museum to learn about Turkey's maritime history.*

Naval Museum QR Code.

✦ **Afternoon**: *Visit the Yıldız Park for a leisurely walk and visit the Yıldız Palace.*

Walk 210 m from the Naval Museum to the Bahcesehir Universitesi tram stop and take tram 30D (Vadi) to Yahya Efendi, then walk 200 m to Yildiz Park.

Yildiz Palace QR Code.

✦ **Evening**: *Enjoy the vibrant nightlife in the Beşiktaş market area with local eateries and bars.*

Walk 260 m from Yildiz Park to the Yahya Efendi tram stop and take tram D2 (Vadi) to Beskitas Meydan, then walk 260 m to Beskitas Market.

Beskitas Market QR Code.

DAY 3: SPORTS AND LEISURE

Day 3.[63]

✦ **Morning**: *Visit Vodafone Park, home to the Beşiktaş football team.*

Vodafone Park QR Code.

✦ **Afternoon**: *Have lunch at a restaurant nearby.*

✦ **Evening**: *Dine at one of the upscale restaurants and try the famous kumpir (stuffed baked potatoes) in Ortaköy, followed by a stroll by the Ortaköy Mosque.*

Day 4.[64]

+ **Morning**: *Enjoy a leisurely breakfast and head to the Ihlamur Palace for a peaceful morning.*

Ihlamur Palace QR Code.

+ **Afternoon**: *Visit the art galleries and small shops in the neighborhood.*

+ **Evening**: *Conclude your visit with a seafood dinner along the Bosphorus, reflecting on the memories made in Beşiktaş.*

Explore the Princes' Islands in one day.[65]

Do you wish to take a break from the city's hustle and bustle? Spend a day at the Princes' Islands.

One Day Trip

✦ **Morning**: *Start your day early by taking a ferry from Kabataş or Üsküdar in Istanbul to Büyükada, the largest of the Princes' Islands. Explore the Büyükada pier area. Visit Aya Yorgi Church and Monastery at the top of Büyükada for outstanding views of the Sea of Marmara.*

Walk 160 m from the pier to the Araba Meydani bus stop and take us BA-2 (Lunapark) to Lunapark, then walk 1.1 km to get to Aya Yorgi Church and Monastery.

Buyukada Pier QR Code.

Aya Yorgi Church and
Monastery QR Code.

✦ **Afternoon**: *Enjoy a leisurely lunch at one of the local seafood restaurants or cafes. The waterfront area offers many dining options with sea views. Stroll down the charming streets of the area or rent a bicycle to explore more remote parts of the island. There are bike rental shops available near the pier. Don't forget to visit the Büyükada Island Museum to learn about the history and culture of the Princes' Islands.*

Buyukada Island Museum QR Code.

✦ **Evening**: *Wind down your day by relaxing on one of the island's beaches. Nakibey Plaj beach comes highly recommended. Alternatively, enjoy a cup of Turkish tea or coffee at a seaside cafe. Catch an evening ferry back to Istanbul. The sunset over the Sea of Marmara can be spectacular.*

From the museum, walk to the Adalar Muzesi bus stop and take bus BA-2 (Araba Meydani) to Mimoza Sokak, then walk 300 m to Nakibey Plaj.

Nakibey Plaj QR Code.

3-DAY ASIAN ISTANBUL TRIP

Explore the Asian side of Istanbul.[66]

The residential side of Istanbul has more to offer than meets the eye. You can cover the Asian side thoroughly in three good days.

DAY 1: KADIKÖY EXPLORATION

Day 1.[67]

+ **Morning**: *Start your day by taking a ferry from Eminönü or Karaköy to Kadıköy. Have a delicious Turkish breakfast before exploring the vibrant Kadıköy market as you shop for fresh produce, spices, and local delicacies. You can also check out the boutiques and shops in the area. Visit the Barış Manço Museum, dedicated to the legendary Turkish musician.*

Walk 400 m to the Kadikoy bus stop and take bus D34 (Bostanci) to Moda Ilkokulu, then walk 450 m to the museum.

Kadikoy Market QR Code.

Baris Manco Museum QR Code.

✦ **Afternoon**: *Have a delicious lunch at Ciya Sofrasi, a restaurant offering a variety of Anatolian dishes. Digest your meal with a leisurely walk along the Moda coast as you stroll its charming streets and parks.*

Address: Caferağa, Güneşli Bahçe Sok, 34710 Kadıköy/İstanbul, Türkiye

✦ **Evening**: *End your first day with a cup of Turkish tea at one of the charming tea houses on Kadife Sokak.*

Day 2.[68]

✦ **Morning**: *Take a ferry from Kadıköy to Üsküdar. Explore the historic district, including the bustling Üsküdar Square. Visit the Mihrimah Sultan Mosque, an architectural gem designed by Mimar Sinan. Proceed to walk along the waterfront and enjoy the view of the Maiden's Tower. Alternatively, you can hire a boat to the tower.*

Walk 160 m from Uskudar Square to get to the Mihrimah Sultan Mosque. The Maiden's Tower is a 1.2 km walk away from the Mosque.

Uskudar Square QR Code.

Mihrimah Sultan Mosque QR Code

Maiden's Tower QR Code.

✦ **Afternoon**: *Have lunch at Yasar Bafra Pide Salonu, a popular restaurant known for its Turkish pide (flatbread). On the Bosphorus shore, you will find Beylerbeyi Palace. This historical Ottoman building resembles a part of some Turkish fairy tale.*

Walk 900 m from the Maiden's Tower to the Uskudar Marmaray bus stop and take bus 12 (Kadikoy) to Halk Caddesi, then walk 100 m to get to Yasar Bafra Pide Salonu. To get to Beylerbeyi Palace, walk 130 m from the restaurant to the Halk Caddesi bus stop and take bus 12 (Kadikoy) to Uskudar Marmary then walk to the Uskudar Camii Onu bus stop and take bus 15B (Kuran Kursu) to the Beylerbeyi Palace stop, then walk 300 m to the Beylerbeyi Palace.

Address: Aziz Mahmut Hüdayi, Halk Cd. No:72, 34672 Üsküdar/İstanbul, Türkiye

Beylerbeyi Palace QR Code.

✦ **Evening**: *Hire a taxi to Kuzguncuk and explore the colorful neighborhood in the light of the setting sun. Have dinner at a local resto and follow it up with a leisurely evening stroll along the Bosphorus.*

DAY 3: NATURE AND RELAXATION

Day 3.⁶⁹

+ **Morning**: *Have an authentic Turkish breakfast. Visit Büyük Çamlıca Park for a relaxing morning surrounded by nature. The views of the city from the park are simply breathtaking. Çamlıca Mosque is nearby, so you may consider visiting it.*

Walk 850 m from Buyuk Camlica Park to get to the Camlica Mosque.

Buyuk Camlica Park QR Code.

Camlica Mosque QR Code.

+ **Afternoon**: *Have lunch at a restaurant near the Mosque.*

+ **Evening**: *Dine near your accommodation and relax and reflect on your trip as you sip a hot cup of coffee.*

THE 3-DAY CULTURAL DELIGHT

Explore the culture of Istanbul in three days.[70]

Istanbul is best known for its arts and culture, and you would be missing out on many delights if you didn't take a full cultural tour of the city. Here's a brief itinerary to get you going.

Day 1.[71]

+ **Morning**: *There is no better start to any cultural tour than exploring the three Istanbul Archaeological Museums near Gulhane Park, housing a vast collection of artifacts from various civilizations. Proceed to Sultanahmet Square for a few hours at the Museum of Turkish and Islamic Arts.*

Walk 850 m from the Istanbul Archaeological Museums to the Museum of Turkish and Islamic Arts.

Museum of Turkish and Islamic Arts QR Code.

✦ **Afternoon**: *Walk back to Gulhane Park for lunch at one of the many good restaurants there. Head to Istanbul Museum of Modern Art, a contemporary art gallery showcasing Turkish and international artists. Its terrace also offers stunning views of the Bosphorus.*

To get to Gulhane Park, walk 1.1 km from the Museum of Turkish and Islamic Arts. From there, walk 600 m to the Gulhane tram stop and take tram T1 (Kabatas) to Tophane, and walk 250 m to get to the Istanbul Museum of Modern Art.

Istanbul Museum of Modern Art QR Code.

✦ **Evening**: *Make your way to the historic Galata Tower, where the long waiting queues will keep you occupied until the evening when the sights of the city from the top seem even more beautiful. End your day by having dinner in the trendy Karaköy or Galata districts.*

Walk 1 km from the Istanbul Museum of Modern Art to the Galata Tower.

Day 2.[72]

+ **Morning**: The Pera Museum should be your first stop on the second day, known for its collection of Orientalist paintings, Anatolian weights and measures, and Kütahya tiles. If you haven't had breakfast yet, you can walk to Istiklal Avenue for brunch at one of the many restaurants there.

+ **Afternoon**: Choose a cozy restaurant in Çiçek Pasajı or the Asmalımescit area for lunch. Visit Salt Galata, an art space and research library in a historic building. It often hosts contemporary art exhibitions and events.

Salt Galata QR Code.

+ **Evening**: Experience Istanbul's street food scene in Karaköy. Try local specialties like simit, balık ekmek (fish sandwich), or Turkish Delight.

DAY 3: KADIKÖY AND ASIAN SIDE

Day 3.[73]

+ **Morning**: *Take a ferry to Kadıköy on the Asian side and spend an hour or two at the market. Wander around the Moda district, known for its trendy boutiques, cafés, and street art.*

Moda District QR Code.

+ **Afternoon**: *There is no better restaurant for having lunch on the Asian side than Ciya Sofrası. Explore Bahariye Street, filled with shops, bookstores, and galleries. Book tickets at Sureyya Opera House nearby if there's a performance.*

To get to Bahariye Street, walk 450 m from Ciya Sofrası. The Sureyya Opera House is a 140 m walk along Bahariye Street.

Address: Caferağa, Güneşli Bahçe Sok, 34710 Kadıköy/İstanbul, Türkiye

Bahariye QR Code.

Sureyya Opera House QR Code.

✦ **Evening**: *Dine at one of the options near the Sureyya Opera House. Taste the delectable Turkish cuisine for the final time before heading back home.*

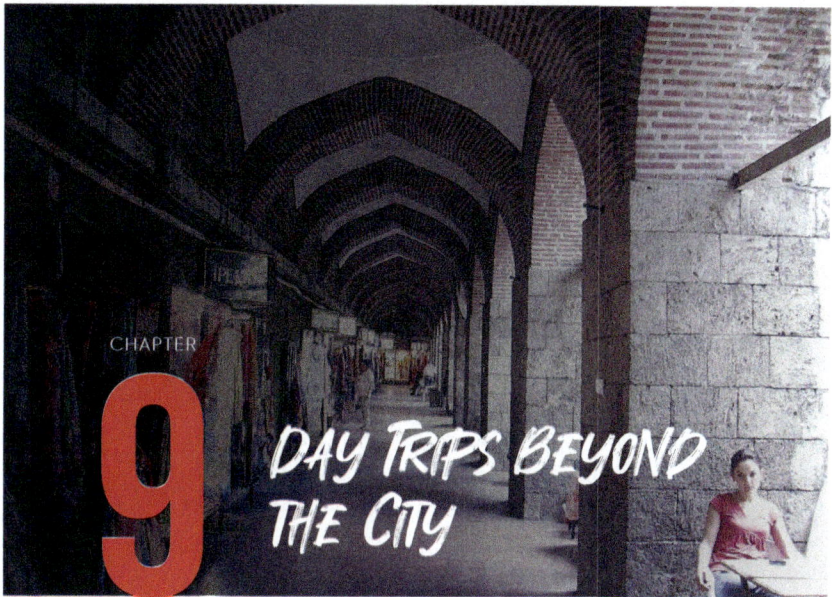

9

DAY TRIPS BEYOND THE CITY

It isn't just Istanbul that is worth visiting. There are a few cities a couple of hours away that you should also add to your itinerary. You will get to explore more Turkish cities and learn about this fascinating country and its culture. This chapter covers Turkey's hidden gems and the fun activities you can do there.

EDIRNE

Edirne was originally called Hadrianopolis after its founder, Roman emperor Hadrian. In 1362, the city was under the control of the Ottomans. From 1413 to 1458, it became the Empire's capital and its cultural, commercial, and administrative center. It was later called Adrianople until 1928 when the Turkish adopted the Latin alphabet and became known as Edirne. The city's long and rich history is evident in its culture and architecture, and you will find traces of the Ottoman Empire on many of its landmarks.

TRAVELING FROM ISTANBUL TO EDIRNE

+ **Bus**: *4 hours and costs $13 to $22.*

+ **Train**: *5 hours and 40 minutes, costing $4 to $7.*

+ **Night Train**: *5 hours and 30 minutes, costing $7 to $13.*

+ **Taxi**: *2 hours and 20 minutes, costing $80 to $100.*

+ **Driving**: *2 hours and 20 minutes and costs $26 to 40$.*

SELIMIYE MOSQUE

Selimiye Mosque is a UNESCO World Heritage site and an Ottoman masterpiece. It should be the first place you visit when you get to Edirne. Sultan Selim II assigned his best architect, Sinan, to build the mosque, which became the pride of the empire. It stands as a testament to the Ottomans' outstanding achievement in architecture.

Selimiye Mosque.[74]

The mosque is a complex. It has a soup kitchen, a market, a school, and a bathhouse. As you arrive at the site, you will be in awe of the mosque's four minarets, intricate design, and octagonal supports that make the building stand out in the middle of the city.

Non-Muslims can enter the mosque and explore its interior design. However, you should take your shoes off, and women should wear a scarf over their heads.

As of the writing of this book, the opening hours are every day from 6:30 AM to 8:30 pm. However, please make sure to double-check the opening hours online should there be any slight changes to their schedule.

Ticket Prices: Entering the mosque is free but you can make a donation if you like.

Address: Meydan, Mimar Sinan Cd., 22020 Edirne Merkez/Edirne, Turkiye.

WRESTLING FESTIVAL

If you visit Edirne in June, you should check Kırkpınar. It is an oil wrestling festival that takes place every year at the end of June or beginning of July and lasts for a week. It usually involves music, dances, and Turkish food. The festival originated in the 1360s during the reign of the Ottoman Empire. Sultan Orhan came up with this idea to keep his soldiers fit and ready for battle. Nowadays, wrestlers train very hard to participate in the festival. However, they must also be good and honest individuals, or they won't get invited. The Kırkpınar Ağası, or master wrestler, invites wrestlers based on their morals and wrestling skills.

Kırkpınar Ağası usually picks his wrestlers in March and sends them a candle with a red base, just like the Ottomans did centuries ago, to notify them that they have been chosen. At the festival, the wrestlers wear a kispet or leather pants. They first perform the Friday prayers to ask for God's blessings before they begin. They then move to Sarayiçi, one of the main destinations in Edirne.

Two thousand wrestlers participate in this event. A yağcı or oiler covers them with olive oil. Bass drums and folk oboes play as the men enter er meydanı or the Field of Contest. This is an excellent experience if you want to immerse yourself in Turkish culture.

Before your visit, check online to see the festival's exact date and book a ticket.

BOAT RIDE ALONG TUNCA RIVER

If you want a romantic and relaxing activity, go on a boat tour along the Tunca River. You will take in Edirne's landmarks and beautiful scenery and enjoy some peace and quiet. You will also get a glimpse of the gorgeous Ottoman architecture, historic bridges, and natural landscape.

Consider taking the guided tour to learn about the city's culture and history.

TRY EDIRNE CUISINE

In Turkey, eating isn't something you do on the go. It is an experience. Don't deprive yourself of sitting in one of Edirne's popular restaurants and enjoy the local cuisine. There are many Turkish dishes to try.

+ **Edirne Ciğer**: *Sliced liver with spices and onions.*

+ **Trakya Köftesi meatball**: *It is made with spices and herbs and served with tomato sauce.*

+ **Peynirli Pide**: *Baked bread with cheese toppings.*

+ **Edirne Bademi**: *A dessert made with rose water, sugar, and almonds.*

+ **Restaurants to Check in Edirne**

+ **Asma Altı Ocakbaşı Restaurant**: *Serves delicious grilled meat.*

Address: İstasyon Mahallesi Şehit Emniyet Müdürü Ertan Nezihi, Turan Dursun Cd. No:56, 22030 Edirne Merkez.

+ **Serenita Restaurant**: *Serves local and international dishes.*

+ **Address:** *Şükrüpaşa, Kıyık Cd. No:254, 22030 Edirne Merkez/ Edirne.*

+ **Hanedan Restaurant**: *Serves seafood and popular Turkish dishes.*

+ **Address:** *Karaağaç, 22100 Edirne Merkez/Edirne.*

+ **Aydın Tava Ciğer**: *Serves local specialty, mezes, and a variety of salads.*

Address: Sabuni, Tahmis Çarşısı Sk. No:8, 22000 Edirne Merkez/Edirne.

BURSA

In the 2nd century, Bursa was ruled by the Roman Empire and was called Prusa ad Olympum. It connected Europe to Asia and acted as the Empire's main trading and cultural center. The Romans built many landmarks around the city that are still standing to this day.

In the 14th century, Bursa became a part of the Ottoman Empire, and Osman I declared it as their first capital. The Ottomans reshaped the city, giving it a new identity. They built one of the city's most popular monuments, the Grand Mosque.

In the 19th century, Bursa underwent an industrial revolution unlike any the world had seen before. Factories were built everywhere in the city, making it an economic powerhouse.

Now, Bursa is a popular destination for locals and tourists alike.

TRAVELING FROM ISTANBUL BURSA

- ✦ **Bus**: 3 hours, costing up to $16.

- ✦ **Rideshare**: 3 hours and 30 minutes, costing $7.

- ✦ **Bus or Train**: 3 hours and 20 minutes, costing $9 to $14.

- ✦ **Taxi**: 1 hour and 30 minutes, costing $110 to $140.

- ✦ **Car**: 1 hour and 30 minutes, costing $17 to $26.

THE GREEN MOSQUE (YESIL CAMI)

The Green mosque is an Ottoman masterpiece. Sultan Celebi Mehmet commissioned architect and commander Haci Ivaz Pasha to build the mosque. It was constructed in 1419 and acted as a court and a government house. Mehmet was buried in a green tomb in the mosque.

The Green Mosque.[75]

The mosque got its name from the green tiles covering its exterior and interior, giving it a magnificent appearance. It has a unique design with a large central dome and eight smaller ones. Underneath the main dome, there is an octagonal pool. The mosque is decorated with marble tiles, making it the first marble Ottoman structure in the city.

The mosque's exterior is breathtaking with its decorative details, beautiful calligraphy, complex stonework, and a blend of turquoise, blue, and green tiles. The interior is equally magnificent. The main prayer hall is adorned with Quranic verses, geometric designs, and floral patterns. The mosque's courtyard is decorated with a central fountain, flowers, and trees. It has a calming atmosphere that offers a welcome break from the crowded and noisy city.

As of the writing of this book, the opening hours are 24 hours every day. However, please make sure to double-check the opening hours online should there be any slight changes to their schedule.

Tickets Price: free.

Address: Yesil, 16360 Yildrim/Bursa, Turkiye.

After touring, you can have a delicious seafood meal at the Drago's Balık Restaurant.

Restaurant Address: Orhantepe Mahallesi, Orhangazi Cad, Mutlu Sk. No:61, 34865 Kartal.

SILK BAZAAR

Turkey is famous for its bazaars. Make the most of your trip and check a bazaar or more in every city you visit. The Silk Bazaar is one of the most popular markets in Bursa. Ottoman Emperor Sultan Bayezid II built it to boost the empire's economy so he could build schools and mosques in Istanbul.

Silk Bazaar.[76]

The bazaar has a two-storied structure surrounding a rectangular courtyard. There is also a one-story building with warehouses, a barn, and a courtyard. The market has three entrances. The north's door has one of the most beautiful designs ever. Stepping into the inner courtyard, you will find a fountain and a mosque above it.

This bazaar is a must-visit if you love history, beautiful architecture, and silk products.

As of the writing of this book, the opening hours are Monday to Saturday from 9 AM to 8 PM. Sunday from 12 PM to 6 PM. However, please make sure to double-check the opening hours online should there be any slight changes to their schedule.

Address: Yesil, 16360 Yildrim/Bursa, Turkiye.

THERMAL BATHS

Bursa is known for its hammams or thermal baths. Enjoy a relaxing and soothing experience to unwind and put all your troubles behind you. People from all over the world visit Bursa for its traditional Turkish baths. The city is distinguished by its hot springs which have been offering people a therapeutic experience for thousands of years. They are rich in sulfur, magnesium, calcium, and many other minerals that induce relaxation, reduce stress, relieve joint and muscle pain, and improve blood circulation.

The baths have various services like skincare treatments, massages, steam rooms, saunas, thermal pools, and more. You will also find multiple bathing experiences, and you can choose the one that suits your needs. The most popular one is the hammam experience, which involves a relaxing massage, scrubbing, steaming, and soaking in Bursa's famous thermal pools. You will feel transformed after this experience and completely relaxed.

Bursa hammams allow you to immerse yourself in Turkish culture and learn about local rituals and traditions. You will get to enjoy the baths' marvelous Ottoman architecture and witness old Turkish bath practices. Most of Bursa's hammams are surrounded by picturesque landscapes and beautiful gardens to enhance the relaxation experience.

CABLE CAR TO ULUDAĞ MOUNTAIN

Your trip to Bursa won't be complete without exploring its breathtaking landscapes. Take a cable car ride to Uludağ Mountain, where you will get to experience the city's beautiful scenery. On your way to the mountain's top, you will see gorgeous valleys, rolling hills, and green forests. There are fun outdoor activities you can engage in when you reach the top, like skiing, snowboarding, or hiking, or you can just sit and take in the natural scenery. If you are looking for a fun and exhilarating adventure, this is the one for you.

The car is called Bursa Teleferik; it has comfortable and spacious cabins, and the ride takes about 25 minutes. Many cafes and restaurants are on the mountain's top, where you can have a cup of coffee or a delicious Turkish dish while enjoying the magnificent landscapes.

The ride to Uludağ Mountain offers a once-in-a-lifetime experience, so take plenty of pictures.

PRINCES' ISLANDS

You are probably wondering what Princes' Islands are doing here when it was already discussed in Chapter 5 as a part of Istanbul. However, reaching the Islands can take an hour or more, depending on the method of transportation you choose, so it fits with this chapter's theme.

Traveling From Istanbul to Princes' Islands

+ **Ferry**: *The trip takes between 75 minutes to two hours.*

VICTORIAN COTTAGES

Princes Islands are all about adventures that transport you from the modern world to the Victorian age. Suppose you are tired of hotels and looking for a different experience. In that case, you can spend a couple of days in a Victorian cottage on Büyükada island. These cottages are perfect for couples looking for a romantic getaway or newlyweds looking for honeymoon ideas.

SAPANCA AND MASUKIYE

Sapanca, usually described as the city of dreams, is in Sakarya in the Marmara Region. Masukiye is located 20 kilometers from Sapanca, north of the Lake. They are two of Turkey's most popular tourist destinations, especially among nature lovers. Wherever you look, you will find beautiful lakes and hills. The weather is usually perfect with fresh and clear air and warm sun. In the spring, flowers like jasmine and lilies bloom, giving the air a beautiful fragrance. In the fall, the view of the yellow leaves on the trees and dropping on the ground looks more beautiful than any painting you have ever seen.

In the winter, the rain falls over the green hill, creating a romantic view perfect for couples or people looking for a peaceful escape to meditate.

The cities are close to Istanbul, and daily tours are available all year long to take you to Sapanca and Masukiye. A car will pick you up from your hotel to spend the day in these magnificent cities.

HIKING

Sapanca Lake is famous for its peaceful and relaxing atmosphere and beautiful scenery, surrounded by nature reserves, parks, rolling hills, and lush forests. Go on a hike while taking in the stunning landscape. The fresh air and perfect weather will make you feel rejuvenated. The place is also great for a morning picnic. Surprise your partner and take them for a romantic picnic where you can enjoy the beautiful scenery.

ORMANYA WILDLIFE

Spend the day with your family at Ormanya Wildlife. It is a breeding center and conservation for lynxes, bears, wolves, leopards, and other endangered animals. Unlike zoos, where you observe animals in captivity, in Ormanya Wildlife, you will see them in their natural habitat. There is also a wide variety of birds for bird-watching enthusiasts. You will find guided tours, a botanical path, a camping area, a caravan, and a bird-watching area. You may glimpse native bird species like vultures, imperial eagles, and steppe eagles. You will also spot mammals like red deer, fallow deer, and wild boars.

You can take your children to the Ormanya Zoo. It is home to 766 animals and offers rocking chairs, benches, and an amphitheater for the comfort of its visitors. You can camp with your family and spend the night watching the stars, playing games, observing the animals and having fun. The zoo has many facilities like a dishwashing area, water, electricity, and showers.

As of the writing of this book, the opening hours are every day from 9 AM to 8 PM and closed on Mondays. However, please make sure to double-check the opening hours online should there be any slight changes to their schedule.

Address: Uzuntarla Mahallesi, 309. Sk. No:88, 41150 Kartepe/Kocaeli, Turkiye.

EXPLORE MASUKIYE

Masukiye offers a relaxing environment and breathtaking scenery. Walk around the village with your friends, family, or partner, and enjoy the picturesque view. Escape from the noisy city and enjoy a calming and quiet atmosphere where you will only hear birds chirping.

İZNIK

Iznik was a part of the Hellenistic, Roman, Byzantine, and Ottoman Empires. In ancient times, the city was called Nicaea. It is considered the third holy city in Christianity after Jerusalem and the Vatican. It is considered an open-air museum due to its rich history and ancient structures created by the civilizations that passed through the city.

One of the most popular parts of the city is its walls. They were built by the Romans and reconstructed by the Byzantines. Nicaea was under the rule of the Byzantines for years until Seljuk's invasion. Afterward, it became a part of the Ottoman Empire, where they established the empire's first school and soup kitchen.

In the 19th century, it became the country's leading trade, art, culture, and education center. However, after the Ottomans colonized Istanbul, they paid more attention to it and ignored Iznik. The city is also famous for pottery and colorful tiles.

There are many legends associated with Iznik. An ancient city similar to Atlantis is believed to be buried under Iznik Lake. There are even rumors among fishermen that their fishing rods and nets get caught on the city's remains. Interestingly, recent discoveries have shown that there may be some truths behind this legend.

TRAVELING FROM ISTANBUL TO IZNIK

+ **Train and Taxi**: *2 hours and 23 minutes, costing $67 to $88.*

+ **Bus**: *3 hours and 30 minutes, costing $10 to $14.*

+ **Taxi**: *1 hour and 38 minutes and costs $90 to $110.*

+ **Car**: *1 hour and 38 minutes, costing $17 to $24.*

HISTORIC MOSQUES

Traces of the Ottoman Empire are found in much of the city's architecture. Explore its historic mosques to learn more about the city's past. One of its most popular is the Haci Ozbek Mosque, the first Ottoman mosque with an inscription that documents its construction. It was built in 1333 by Haci Özbek bin Muhammed, whom

Haci Ozbek Mosque.[79]

the mosque is named after. It is a brick architecture with mixed stones and a square plan. The Hagia Sophia, Green Mosque, and Suleymaniye Mosque are some mosques you should visit in Iznik.

Address: Esrefzade, 16860 Iznik/Bursa, Turkiye.

IZNIK LAKE

Iznik Lake is the fifth-largest lake in Turkey and the largest in Marmara. The lake is associated with myths and legends since many believe the lost city is under water. In 2014, archaeologist Mustafa Sahin and his team discovered the remains of a fifth-century basilica. Take a canoe and explore the remains yourself. You can easily see them from above water, provided the water is clear, and the weather is good. Afterward, you can enjoy a seafood meal at Nihat'ın Yeri Balık Restaurant or a local dish at Kaptan'ın Yeri.

Iznik Lake.[77]

N.B. All the prices, working hours, and addresses mentioned here were from the time of writing this book. Please double-check this information online before your trip.

Istanbul is surrounded by many cities that offer excellent and unique experiences. Whether you are looking for a relaxing holiday or a fun adventure, you will find something that caters to your needs. Just like Istanbul, every city mentioned here is worth exploring. Don't forget to take pictures of the beautiful scenery and landmarks.

BONUS CHAPTER: USEFUL SURVIVAL PHRASES

When it comes to prominent regions in Turkey, like Istanbul, English is widely spoken throughout. It is even taught as a second language in schools, and the employees at tourist-specific places like hotels, restaurants, and ticket counters can speak English fluently. Nonetheless, it's better to learn a few phrases of Istanbul's (and Turkey's) official language, Turkish, before heading to the city. After all, on a foreign trip, the locals expect you to understand their language instead of them understanding yours. Learning the local language of the place you're visiting is also a common courtesy.

Learn a few survival phrases before your trip to Istanbul.[78]

BASIC TURKISH PHRASES

This section translates the phrases you'll hear most often during your trip. Also, you will need to know these to socialize with the locals or in case of an emergency.

COMMON WORDS AND PHRASES

+ **Hello** - *Merhaba (Mehr-hah-bah)*

+ **Goodbye** - *Hoşça kal (Hoh-shah kahl)*

+ **Please** - *Lütfen (Loot-fen)*

+ **Thank you** - *Teşekkür ederim (Teh-shehk-koor eh-deh-reem)*

+ **Yes** - *Evet (Eh-vet)*

+ **No** - *Hayır (Hah-yuhr)*

+ **Excuse me / I'm sorry** - *Afedersiniz (Ahf-feh-dehr-sin-iz)*

GREETINGS

+ **Hi** - *Selam (Seh-lahm)*

+ **Good morning** - *Günaydın (Goo-nahy-dun)*

+ **Good day / Hello** (used throughout the day) - *İyi günler (Ee-yee goon-lehr)*

+ **Good evening** - *İyi akşamlar (Ee-yee ahk-shahm-lar)*

+ **Good night** - *İyi geceler (Ee-yee geh-jeh*

+ *-lehr)*

+ **How are you?** - *Nasılsın? (Nah-suhl-suhn)*

+ **Thank you** - *Teşekkür ederim (Teh-shehk-kur ed-air-im)*

+ **You're welcome** - *Rica ederim (Ree-jah ed-air-im)*

+ **Welcome** (formal) - *Hoş geldiniz (Hosh gel-deen-ez)*

GOODBYES

The Turkish have many ways to say "goodbye."

✦ **Goodbye** *(said by the person who is leaving)* - *Hoşça kal (Hosh-cha kal)*

✦ **Goodbye** *(said to the person who is leaving)* - *Güle güle (Goo-leh goo-leh)*

✦ **Goodbye** *(used when the person leaving is not expected to return soon)* - *Allahaısmarladık (Ah-lah-hah-ee-smar-lah-dik)*

✦ **Goodbye** *(used when you expect to see the person again)* - *Görüşürüz (Goo-roo-shur-uz)*

✦ **May it come easy** *(used when someone is about to start a task or journey, equivalent to "good luck")* - *Kolay gelsin (Koh-lahy gel-sin)*

NUMBERS

✦ **One** - *Bir (beer)*

✦ **Two** - *İki (ee-kee)*

✦ **Three** - *Üç (uhch)*

✦ **Four** - *Dört (durt)*

✦ **Five** - *Beş (besh)*

✦ **Six** - *Altı (ahl-too)*

✦ **Seven** - *Yedi (yeh-dee)*

✦ **Eight** - *Sekiz (seh-keez)*

✦ **Nine** - *Dokuz (doh-kooz)*

✦ **Ten** - *On (on)*

DAYS OF THE WEEK

✦ **Monday** - *Pazartesi (Pah-zahr-teh-see)*

✦ **Tuesday** - *Salı (Sah-luh)*

✦ **Wednesday** - *Çarşamba (Char-shahm-bah)*

✦ **Thursday** - *Perşembe (Pehr-shem-beh)*

✦ **Friday** - *Cuma (Joo-mah)*

✦ **Saturday** - *Cumartesi (Joo-mar-teh-see)*

✦ **Sunday** - *Pazar (Pah-zahr)*

SMALL TALK

Once you have exchanged pleasantries, it's time to start with a bit of small talk to make them comfortable around you.

✦ **Good, thank you** - İyi, teşekkür ederim (Ee-yee, teh-shehk-kur ed-air-im)

✦ **What is your name?** - Adınız ne? (Ah-din-uz neh)

✦ **My name is...** - Benim adım... (Beh-neem ah-dum...)

✦ **Nice to meet you** - Memnun oldum (Mem-noon ol-dum)

✦ **What are you doing?** - Ne yapıyorsunuz? (Neh yah-puh-yor-soon-uz)

✦ **Nice to meet you** (formal) - Sizi tanıdığıma memnun oldum (See-zee tah-nuh-duh-yee-mah mem-noon ol-dum)

✦ **Which city are you from?** - Hangi şehirden geliyorsunuz? (Han-gee sheh-eer-den gel-ee-yor-soon-uz)

✦ **How is the weather?** - Hava nasıl? (Hah-vah nah-suhl)

✦ **It's a beautiful day, isn't it?** - Güzel bir gün, değil mi? (Goo-zel beer goon, deh-eel mee)

PHRASES FOR SOCIALIZING

These are advanced phrases you can use to transition from small talk to a meaningful conversation.

✦ **Nice to meet you** - Tanıştığımıza memnun oldum (Tah-neesh-ti-mi-zah mem-noon ol-dum)

✦ **What have you been up to lately?** - Neler yapıyorsun bu aralar? (Neh-ler yah-puh-yor-soon boo ah-rah-lar)

✦ **Have you been here before?** - Buraya daha önce geldin mi? (Boo-rah-yah dah-ha urhn-jay gel-din mi)

✦ **Have you traveled and seen interesting places?** - Gezip gördüğün yerler var mı? (Geh-zip gur-doo-yun yer-ler var muh)

✦ **How are you enjoying this event?** - Bu etkinlikte nasıl eğleniyorsunuz? (Boo et-keen-leek-te nah-suhl eh-len-ee-yor-soo-nooz)

✦ **Have we met before?** - Daha önce buluştuk mu? (Dah-ha urhn-jay boo-loosh-took mu)

+ **Would you like to spend time together?** - *Birlikte vakit geçirmek ister misin? (Beer-leek-te va-keet gey-er-mek is-ter mee-sin)*

+ **I would like to get to know you better** - *Sizi daha yakından tanımak isterim (See-zee dah-ha yah-kin-dan tah-nuh-mak is-ter-eem)*

PHRASES FOR RESTAURANTS

As long as you know the names of the Turkish dishes and what they contain, you will be fine with just the common phrases at restaurants. If you don't, here are a few valuable translations that will help.

+ **I would like to make a reservation** - *Masa ayırtmak istiyorum (Mah-sah ah-yurt-mahk is-tee-yor-um)*

+ **The menu, please** - *Menü lütfen (Meh-noo loot-fen)*

+ **Can I have the menu, please?** - *Menüyü alabilir miyim, lütfen? (Meh-noo-yoo ahl-ah-bee-leer mee-yeem, loot-fen)*

+ **Are you ready to order now?** - *Şu an hazır mısınız? (Shoo ahn hah-zeer mees-in-uz)*

+ **What is today's special?** - *Bugünün spesiyali nedir? (Boo-goon-oon speh-syah-lee ned-eer)*

+ **I would like...** - *Ben... istiyorum. (Ben... is-tee-yor-um)*

+ **I would like to try this** - *Bunu denemek istiyorum (Boo-noo den-em-ek is-tee-yor-um)*

+ **A bottle of water, please** - *Bir şişe su lütfen (Beer shee-she soo loot-fen)*

+ **The check, please** - *Hesap lütfen (Heh-sahp loot-fen)*

+ **Thank you, it was delicious** - *Teşekkür ederim, çok lezzetliydi (Teh-shehk-kur ed-air-im, chook lez-zet-lee-dee)*

+ **I will leave a tip** - *Bahşiş bırakacağım (Bah-shish bur-ah-kah-ahm)*

PHRASES FOR PUBLIC TRANSPORT

The signs for hailing a taxi or indicating the number of tickets are the same in Turkey. However, there may be times when you need to speak to make them understand your requirements.

+ **Taxi** - *Taksi (Tahk-see)*

+ **Where is the bus?** - *Otobüs nerede? (O-to-booz neh-reh-deh)*

+ **Where is the train station?** - *Tren istasyonu nerede? (Tren ees-tah-yo-noo neh-reh-deh)*

+ **I have a plane ticket** - *Uçak biletim var (Oo-jak bee-let-eem var)*

+ **I would like to buy a ticket** - *Bilet almak istiyorum (Bee-let al-mahk is-tee-yor-um)*

+ **On which platform?** - *Hangi peronda? (Han-gee peh-ron-da)*

+ **How long does it take?** - *Ne kadar sürer? (Neh ka-dar soo-rer)*

+ **Which stop should I get off at?** - *Hangi durakta inmeliyim? (Han-gee doo-rak-ta een-mel-eem)*

+ **Where is the car rental office?** - *Araba kiralama ofisi nerede? (Ah-ra-bah kee-rah-lah-mah oh-fee-see neh-reh-deh)*

+ **The destination is**... - *Gidilecek yer... (Gee-dee-leh-jek yer...)*

PHRASES FOR SHOPPING

The Turkish people are hardcore bargainers. You cannot hope to test your bargaining skills if you do not understand what is being said in Istanbul's markets.

+ **Store** - *Mağaza (Mah-gah-zah)*

+ **I want to go shopping** - *Alışveriş yapmak istiyorum (Ah-lish-veh-reesh yap-mahk is-tee-yor-um)*

+ **How much is it?** - *Ne kadar? (Neh ka-dar)*

+ **Can I buy this?** - *Bunu alabilirim mi? (Boo-noo ah-lah-bee-lee-reem mee)*

+ **Is there a discount?** - *İndirim var mı? (In-dee-reem var muh)*

+ **Can we negotiate the price?** - *Fiyat pazarlığı yapabilir miyiz? (Fee-yat pah-zar-luh-uh yap-a-bee-leer mee-eez)*

- **What size?** - *Hangi beden? (Han-gee bed-en)*

- **What are the color options?** - *Renk seçenekleri neler? (Renk se-cheh-nek-leh-ree neh-lair)*

- **Is this item on sale?** - *Bu ürün indirimde mi? (Boo oor-oon in-dee-rem-deh mee)*

- **Cash or credit card?** - *Nakit veya kredi kartı mı? (Nah-keet yeh-ah kreh-dee kar-tuh muh)*

EMERGENCY PHRASES

You will be immediately assisted if you shout for "help" in English in a public place in Istanbul. However, it is better to know a few emergency phrases, just in case you end up in a remote part of the city.

- **Help!** - *Yardım! (Yar-duhm)*

- **Emergency!** - *Acil durum! (Ah-jeel doh-room)*

- **Call an ambulance, please** - *Ambulans çağırın, lütfen (Ahm-boo-lahns chah-ee-reen, loot-fen)*

- **Call the police, please** - *Polis çağırın, lütfen (Poh-lees chah-ee-reen, loot-fen)*

- **Call the fire department, please** - *İtfaiye çağırın, lütfen (Eet-fah-yeh chah-ee-reen, loot-fen)*

- **I need help** - *Benim yardıma ihtiyacım var (Beh-neem yar-duh-mah eet-yah-jah-jum var)*

- **I am lost** - *Kayboldum (Kai-bold-um)*

- **There is a fire** - *Yangın var (Yahn-ghun var)*

- **There has been a theft** - *Hırsızlık oldu (Her-seez-lik ol-doo)*

- **Call a doctor, please** - *Doktor çağırın, lütfen (Dok-tor chah-ee-reen, loot-fen)*

TIPS FOR LEARNING TURKISH

Turkish is much more challenging to grasp than other European languages, especially for US natives. Many of its pronunciations don't exist in the English language. Simply reading out the phrases above will help you to a point, but beyond that, it's up to you to survive with your advanced language skills in Istanbul. Here are a few tips that will help.

Start with the Basics

Begin by learning the Turkish alphabet and basic pronunciation. Familiarize yourself with the unique sounds of the language. Recite the numbers and the days of the week thoroughly.

Use Language Learning Apps

Utilize language learning apps like Duolingo, Babbel, or Memrise to practice vocabulary, grammar, and phrases.

Take Formal Courses

If you are going to spend a few days in Istanbul, consider enrolling in a Turkish language course, either in person or online. Many platforms offer structured lessons and interactive activities.

Practice Regularly

Consistency is key. Set aside dedicated time each day to practice Turkish, whether reading, listening, or speaking.

Immerse Yourself

Surround yourself with the language as much as possible. Watch Turkish movies, listen to Turkish music, and follow Turkish social media accounts. This exposure will help you get used to the natural flow of the language.

Find Language Exchange Partners

Connect with native Turkish speakers or language exchange partners to practice speaking. Websites like Tandem or HelloTalk can help you find language exchange opportunities.

Read Turkish Materials

Start with simple texts, children's books, or online articles. Progress to Turkish myths and fairy tales, improving your language and giving you a basic understanding of Istanbul's culture.

Use Flashcards

Create flashcards to memorize vocabulary and phrases. Quiz yourself regularly to reinforce what you've learned.

Join Language Learning Communities

Participate in online forums or communities where learners share resources, experiences, and tips. Engaging with others can provide motivation and valuable insights.

Watch Turkish TV Shows and Movies with Subtitles

Watching Turkish content with English subtitles can help you improve your listening skills and comprehension. Movies like Winter Sleep (2014) and Once Upon a Time in Anatolia (2011) provide an immersive experience.

Practice Speaking Aloud

Don't be shy about speaking aloud, even if you're practicing alone. This helps improve pronunciation and fluency.

Be Patient and Persistent

Language learning takes time, and learning Turkish is no different, so be patient with yourself. Celebrate small victories and stay persistent in your efforts.

CONCLUSION

The largest city in Turkey has a lot to offer for every type of traveler. History buffs can revel in its ancient Ottoman reign. Culture enthusiasts can get a taste of both Middle Eastern and Western cultures, with a bit of Asian sprinkled in. The religiously inclined have a number of historic mosques and temples to visit. And the creatives are bound to enjoy the art and architecture of the place.

To summarize the book, it starts with giving a brief overview of Istanbul, its geographical location, the demeanor of its people, the city's background history, its culture and traditions, sports and leisure, and so much more. It's like showing the highlights of the game before watching it live.

The journey to the city begins in the next chapter with details about two of its airports, Istanbul Airport and Sabiha Gökçen International Airport. The various navigation options and the numerous transportation options are described from the airports to the city's main areas.

Then begins the actual tour of Istanbul, as you explore the European side of the city first. Most of the city's gems lie in the Sultanahmet area, from the world-famous Hagia Sophia to the picturesque Blue Mosque. No matter how long you stay in Istanbul, visiting Sultanahmet should always be at the top of your list. Other equally mesmerizing districts like Bakırköy and Sarıyer also should not be missed.

The Asian side of Istanbul may be mostly residential. Still, it has several unique sights that cannot be seen anywhere else, like the Aydos Hill in Sancaktepe and the Anadolu Hisarı fortress in Beykoz. Then there are the Princes' Islands, which take you to a different world altogether. They are much more peaceful and serene than the noisy streets of Istanbul.

Kadıköy and Üsküdar are major tourist hotspots on the Asian side, with sights like the dynamic Moda neighborhood and the legendary Maiden's Tower. The European side has its own set of hotspots to boast about. The Galata Tower in Beyoğlu may have ultra-long queues, but the wait is well worth the views from

the top. Then there's the Dolmabahçe Palace in Beşiktaş and the haggler's heaven, the Grand Bazaar, in Fatih. The Atatürk Museum in Şişli also should not be missed.

The final pages of the book detail different itineraries and programs based on your travel duration and budget. A few of the magnificent regions beyond Istanbul are also explored, perfect for a day trip away from the city's cacophony. The book concludes with a long list of useful survival phrases in Turkish to enhance your trip to Istanbul.

APPENDIX

This section includes an A to Z list of all attractions, sights, places, museums, etc., mentioned throughout the book, with reference to the pages on which they are mentioned.

Adalar Museum, Büyükada - Mentioned in Chapter 5

Akaretler Sıraevler area, Beşiktaş - Mentioned in Chapter 7

Akasya Acıbadem Shopping Mall, Üsküdar - Mentioned in Chapter 6

Akpinar village, European Istanbul - Mentioned in Chapter 2

Akvaryum Bay beach, Heybeliada - Mentioned in Chapter 5

Anadolu Hisarı fortress, Beykoz - Mentioned in Chapter 4

Antika Pazarı market, Üsküdar - Mentioned in Chapter 6

Aqua Green Beach, Heybeliada - Mentioned in Chapter 5

Aqueduct of Valens, Fatih - Mentioned in Chapter 3

Ataşehir area, Asian Istanbul - Mentioned in Chapter 4

Atatürk Forest, Bakırköy - Mentioned in Chapter 3

Atatürk Museum, Şişli - Mentioned in Chapter 7

Atlas Cinema, Beyoğlu - Mentioned in Chapter 7

Aya Triada Seminary, Heybeliada - Mentioned in Chapter 5

Aya Yani Church, Burgazada - Mentioned in Chapter 5

Aya Yorgi Cliff Church, Heybeliada - Mentioned in Chapter 5

Aya Yorgi Monastery, Büyükada - Mentioned in Chapter 5

Ayazma beach, Kınalıada - Mentioned in Chapter 5

Aydos Forest, Sancaktepe - Mentioned in Chapter 4

Aydos Hill, Sancaktepe - Mentioned in Chapter 4

Bagdat Avenue, Maltepe - Mentioned in Chapter 4

Bakırköy district, European Istanbul - Mentioned in Chapter 3

Balat area, Fatih - Mentioned in Chapter 3

Barlar Sokağı street, Kadıköy - Mentioned in Chapter 6

Başakşehir district, European Istanbul - Mentioned in Chapter 3

Basilica Cistern, Sultanahmet - Mentioned in Chapter 3

Bayraklı Monastery, Burgazada - Mentioned in Chapter 5

Bayrampaşa district, European Istanbul - Mentioned in Chapter 3

Bebek Art Street, Beşiktaş - Mentioned in Chapter 7

Belgrad Forest, Sarıyer - Mentioned in Chapter 3

Beşiktaş district, European Istanbul - Mentioned in Chapters 1, 5, 7, and 8

Beşiktaş Square - Mentioned in Chapter 7

Bet Yaakov Synagogue, Heybeliada - Mentioned in Chapter 5

Beykoz district, Asian Istanbul - Mentioned in Chapter 4

Beylerbeyi Palace, Üsküdar - Mentioned in Chapter 3

Beyoğlu district, European Istanbul - Mentioned in Chapters 1 and 7

Blue Mosque, Sultanahmet - Mentioned in Chapters 1, 3, and 6

Boğa Heykeli statue, Kadıköy - Mentioned in Chapter 6

Bosphorus Bridge, Ortaköy - Mentioned in Chapter 3

Bosphorus Strait - Mentioned in all Chapters

Bostancı area, Kadıköy - Mentioned in Chapter 5

Burgazada Island, Sea of Marmara - Mentioned in Chapters 5 and 9

Burgazada Terrace cafe, Burgazada - Mentioned in Chapter 5

Bursa city, south of Istanbul - Mentioned in Chapter 9

Büyükada Island, Sea of Marmara - Mentioned in Chapters 5 and 9

Byzantine ruins, Kınalıada - Mentioned in Chapter 5

Cam Limani Bay, Heybeliada - Mentioned in Chapter 5

Çamlıca Tepesi hill, Üsküdar - Mentioned in Chapter 6

Cevahir Mall, Şişli - Mentioned in Chapter 7

Chora Church, Fatih - Mentioned in Chapter 7

Çırağan Palace Kempinski hotel, Beşiktaş - Mentioned in Chapter 3

Degirmentepe Hill, Heybeliada - Mentioned in Chapter 5

Dolmabahçe Palace, Beşiktaş - Mentioned in Chapter 7

Ecole St. Pierre Hotel, Galata Tower - Mentioned in Chapter 3

Edirne city, northwest of Istanbul - Mentioned in Chapter 9

Eminönü area, Fatih - Mentioned in Chapters 1, 3, and 5

Ergun Patisseria, Burgazada - Mentioned in Chapter 5

Eskibag Teras Restaurant, Büyükada - Mentioned in Chapter 5

Eyüp Sultan Mosque, Eyüpsultan - Mentioned in Chapter 3

Eyüpsultan district, European Istanbul - Mentioned in Chapter 3

Fatih district, European Istanbul - Mentioned in Chapters 1 and 7

Fener area, Fatih - Mentioned in Chapter 3

Galata Antique Bazaar, Beyoğlu - Mentioned in Chapter 7

Galata Bridge, Beyoğlu - Mentioned in Chapters 1 and 3

Galata Tower, Beyoğlu - Mentioned in Chapter 7

Gezi Park, Beyoğlu - Mentioned in Chapter 7

Golden Horn waterway - Mentioned in Chapters 1 and 3

Grand Bazaar, Fatih - Mentioned in Chapters 1 and 7

Green Mosque, Bursa - Mentioned in Chapter 9

Gülhane Park, Eminönü - Mentioned in Chapter 3

Haci Ozbek Mosque, İznik - Mentioned in Chapter 9

Hafız Ahmet Paşa Market, Üsküdar - Mentioned in Chapter 6

Hagia Sophia mosque, Sultanahmet - Mentioned in Chapters 1, 3, and 6

Hagios Nikolaos Church, Heybeliada - Mentioned in Chapter 5

Halik Koyu beach, Büyükada - Mentioned in Chapter 5

Halk Bahçesi garden, Kadıköy - Mentioned in Chapter 6

Halki Seminary, Heybeliada - Mentioned in Chapter 5

Hamidiye mosque, Büyükada - Mentioned in Chapter 5

Here's another book by Captivating Travels that you might like

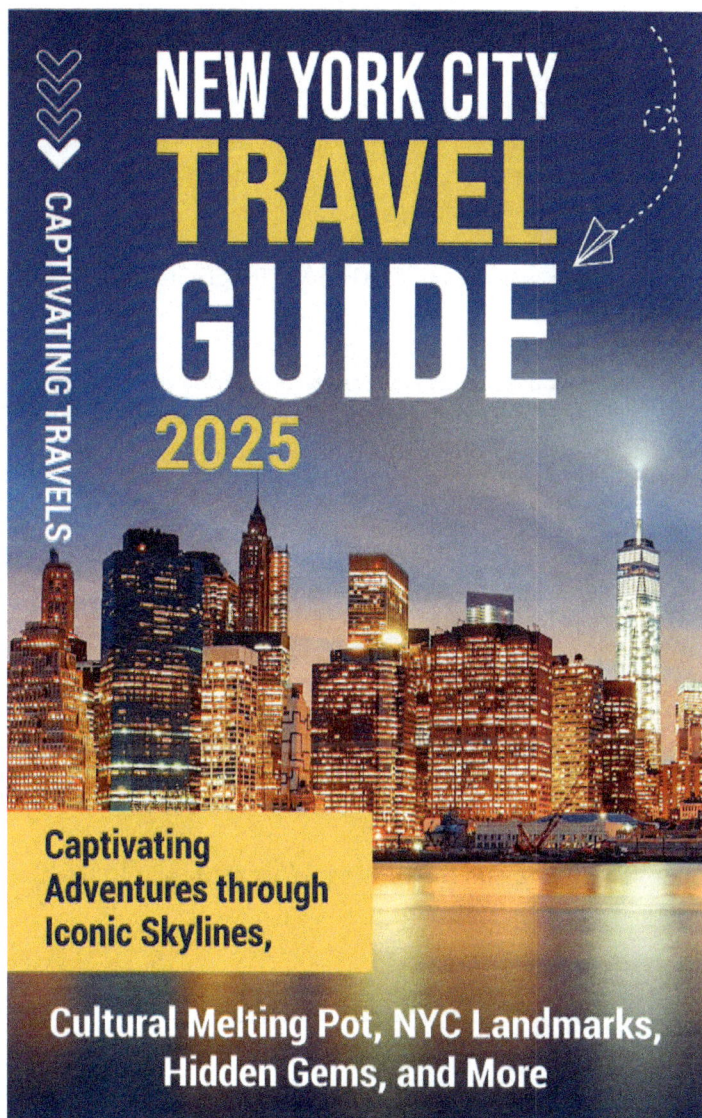

NEW YORK CITY TRAVEL GUIDE 2025

CAPTIVATING TRAVELS

Captivating Adventures through Iconic Skylines,

Cultural Melting Pot, NYC Landmarks, Hidden Gems, and More

Welcome Aboard, Discover
Your Limited-Time Free Bonus!

Hello, traveler! Welcome to the Captivating Travels family, and thanks for grabbing a copy of this book! Since you've chosen to join us on this journey, we'd like to offer you something special.

Check out the link below for a FREE Ultimate Travel Checklist eBook & Printable PDF to make your travel planning stress-free and enjoyable.

But that's not all - you'll also gain access to our exclusive email list with even more free e-books and insider travel tips. Well, what are you waiting for? Click the link below to join and embark on your next adventure with ease.

Access your bonus here: https://livetolearn.lpages.co/ checklist/

Or, Scan the QR code!

REFERENCES

10 Reasons To Visit Istanbul | istanbul.com. (2022, November 16). Istanbul. com. https://istanbul.com/city-life/10-reasons-to-visit-istanbul

A Guide To Contemporary Art Galleries And Museums In Istanbul (2023). (2023, April 10). A GUIDE to CONTEMPORARY ART GALLER-IES and MUSEUMS in ISTANBUL. https://istanbul.tips/discovering-istan-buls-art-scene-a-guide-to-art-contemporary-galleries-and-museums/#A_Brief_History_of_Istanbuls_Art_Scene_and_Its_Importance_in_the_Citys_Culture

Amanda Briney. (2018). A Brief History of Constantinople/Istanbul, Turkey. ThoughtCo. https://www.thoughtco.com/istanbul-was-once-constantino-ple-1435547

Amino, M. (n.d.). İstanbul Traditions | Erasmus experience Istanbul. Erasmusu. com. https://erasmusu.com/en/erasmus-istanbul/erasmus-experiences/istan-bul-traditions-937823

Arberk Bozoglu, F. (2022, January 27). The Top 13 Foods To Try In Istanbul in 2023. The Tour Guy. https://thetourguy.com/travel-blog/turkey/istanbul/top-foods-to-try-in-istanbul-this-year/

Bileta, V. (2023, April 5). What Was the Nika Riot? TheCollector. https://www.thecollector.com/what-was-the-nika-riot/

culturetrip. (2017, February 21). Turkish Traditions You'll Find Fascinating. Culture Trip. https://theculturetrip.com/europe/turkey/articles/8-turkish-tra-ditions-youll-find-fascinating

Does Muslim Turkey Belong in Christian Europe? (2005, January 13). Pew Research Center's Religion & Public Life Project. https://www.pewresearch.org/religion/2005/01/13/does-muslim-turkey-belong-in-christian-europe/

Drew (PhD), C. (2022, October 29). 10 Turkish People Physical Characteris-tics and Traits (2023). Helpfulprofessor.com. https://helpfulprofessor.com/turkish-people-physical-characteristics/

Editör. (2021, December 21). Traditional and Cultural Practices in Turkey You Should Know. Nevita. https://www.nevitaint.com/blog/unique-turkish-customs-and-traditions-that-youll-find-interesting/

Farah. (2023, May 1). Top 15 Things to Do in Istanbul's Asian Side. Discover Walks Blog. https://discoverwalks.com/blog/istanbul/top-10-things-to-do-in-istanbuls-asian-side/

Firas. (2019, November 22). TOP 20 Most Visited Cities in the World (2022 Updated). Travelness.com. https://travelness.com/most-visited-cities-in-the-world

Hattam, J. (2023, April 15). How to get around in Istanbul. Lonely Planet. https://lonelyplanet.com/articles/getting-around-istanbul

History of Istanbul - From ancient Constantinople to Istanbul. (n.d.). Www. introducingistanbul.com. https://introducingistanbul.com/history

Istanbul Art Scene-Check it out! (2013, July 16). Where's Bosco. https://wheresbosconow.com/istanbul-art-scene-check-it-out/

Istanbul Crossroads - Geography & History. (n.d.). Smithsonian Folklife Festival. https://festival.si.edu/2002/the-silk-road/istanbul-geography-and-history/smithsonian

Istanbul Cultural Center | istanbul.com. (2022, September 29). Istanbul.com. https://istanbul.com/city-life/istanbul-cultural-center

Istanbul's Asian side. (2020, June 14). TOOISTANBUL, Visit Istanbul, Planning Stay at Istanbul. https://tooistanbul.com/en/istanbuls-asian-side/#:~:text=One%20of%20the%20main%20%E2%80%9Cattractions

Jacobs, J. (2014, May 12). Things You Should Know about Turks. GlobalCom PR Network. https://www.gcpr.net/blog/things-you-should-know-about-turks/

Jones, R. (n.d.). Dishes that you have got to try in Istanbul. Times of India Travel. https://timesofindia.indiatimes.com/travel/eating-out/dishes-that-you-have-got-to-try-in-istanbul/articleshow/51821997.cms

LAU, S. (2023, October 20). 18 Amazing Things Istanbul Is Known For! - The Turkey Traveler. 18 Amazing Things Istanbul Is Known For! https://theturkey-traveler.com/what-is-istanbul-known-for/

Lifestyle in Istanbul | Expat Arrivals. (n.d.). Www.expatarrivals.com. https://www.expatarrivals.com/europe/turkey/istanbul/lifestyle-istanbul

Lynn. (2022, February 19). 10 Famous People from Istanbul. https://www.discoverwalks.com/blog/istanbul/10-famous-people-from-istanbul/

Max. (2020, September 21). 10 Things to Know About Turkish Traditions and Culture. Property Turkey | Real Estate for Sale | Apartments Villas Investment. https://www.realestateallturkey.com/turkish-traditions-and-culture

Muller, J. (2023, June 20). Istanbul's Unmatched Diversity. Digital Global Traveler. https://medium.com/digital-global-traveler/istanbuls-unmatched-diversity-8525110d24f5

MURPHY, L. (n.d.). 27 Reasons Istanbul Residents Believe They Live in the Best City on Earth. Matador Network. https://matadornetwork.com/notebook/27-reasons-istanbul-residents-believe-live-best-city-earth/

onenationtravel. (2023, April 12). What's Istanbul famous for? | The Complete Guide to Istanbul. What's Istanbul Famous For? https://www.onenationtravel.com/whats-istanbul-famous-for/#:~:text=Istanbul%2C%20a%20city%20that%20straddles

Sansal, B. (n.d.). History of Istanbul - All About Istanbul. Www.allaboutistanbul.com. http://www.allaboutistanbul.com/history.html

Sarah-Jane. (2023, January 11). Discovering The 39 Districts In Istanbul, Türkiye. Chasing the Donkey. https://chasingthedonkey.com/39-districts-in-istanbul-turkiye/

Sawyer, J. (2014, December 2). The 10 Most Authentic Tea Gardens In Istanbul. Culture Trip. https://theculturetrip.com/europe/turkey/articles/istanbul-s-10-authentic-tea-gardens-and-outdoor-cafes

Sports - All About Istanbul. (n.d.). Www.allaboutistanbul.com. http://www.allaboutistanbul.com/sports.html

The Best Bazaars in Istanbul. (n.d.). AFAR Media. https://www.afar.com/travel-tips/the-best-bazaars-in-istanbul

The Geography Of Istanbul | istanbul.com. (2022, November 16). Istanbul.com. https://istanbul.com/city-life/the-geography-of-istanbul

The Things You Should Know About Istanbul. (n.d.). The Things You Should Know about Istanbul. https://www.enjoytravel.com/ca/travel-news/interesting-facts/facts-about-istanbul

TheOtherTour. (2013, January 19). Diversity of Istanbul. The Other Tour. https://theothertour.com/diversity-of-istanbul/#:~:text=A%202008%20report%20prepared%20by

Traditional Turkish Handicrafts and Their History - GoTürkiye. (n.d.). Goturkiye.com. https://goturkiye.com/traditional-turkish-handicrafts-and-their-history

Yalav-Heckeroth, F. (2017, December 14). Reasons Why You'll Fall In Love With Turkey's People. Culture Trip. https://theculturetrip.com/europe/turkey/articles/10-reasons-why-youll-fall-in-love-with-turkeys-people

About | Istanbul Sabiha Gokcen International Airport | Routes. (n.d.). Www.routesonline.com. https://routesonline.com/airports/6063/istanbul-sabiha-gokcen-international-airport/about/

Ateş, S. (n.d.). Gates and Terminals of Istanbul and Sabiha Gokcen Airport. Istanbul Guide and Travel Tips. https://goodistanbulguide.com/gates-and-terminals-of-istanbul-and-sabiha-gokcen-airport/

BAGGAGE DEPOSIT. (n.d.). BAGGAGE DEPOSIT. https://sabihagokcen.aero/passengers-and-visitors/before-flight/baggage-deposit#:~:text=Baggage%20storage%20operates%2024%2F7,level%20of%20the%20passenger%20terminal.

Entry Requirements & Customs in Istanbul | Frommer's. (n.d.). Www.frommers.com. https://www.frommers.com/destinations/istanbul/planning-a-trip/entry-requirements--customs

Guide to Sabiha Gokcen International Airport [SAW] - 2024. (2023, May 3). Introduction to Sabiha Gokcen International Airport [SAW]. https://istanbu-lairporttransfer.gen.tr/sabiha-gokcen-international-airport/

How to get from Istanbul Airport to Taksim Square. (n.d.). Istanbul International Airport https://istanbul-international-airport.com/transportation/airport-transfer-to-taksim/

INFORMATION DESK. (n.d.). INFORMATION DESK. https://sabihagokcen.aero/passengers-and-visitors/passenger-guide/terminal-guide/information-desk

ISTANBUL AIRPORT LUGGAGE STORAGE. (n.d.). ISTANBUL AIRPORT LUGGAGE STORAGE. https://airport.online/istanbul-airport/en/istanbul-airport-luggage-storage

Istanbul International Airport (IST) | The New Istanbul Airport. (n.d.). Istanbul International Airport. https://istanbul-international-airport.com/

Navigating The New Istanbul Airport (IST): Terminals, Gates Maps & Minimum Connection Time. (2023, March 21). NAVIGATING the NEW ISTANBUL AIRPORT (IST): TERMINALS, GATES MAPS, & MINIMUM CONNECTION TIME. https://istanbul.tips/navigating-the-new-istanbul-airport-ist-a-guide-to-the-maps-transportation-and-terminals/#Terminal_Navigating_Tips_International_vs_Domestic_Flights_Airport_Istanbul

Public Transport Istanbul 2022 | Prices, Maps, Lines, Airports. (2020, September 4). Complete Guide to Public Transport in Istanbul. https://istanbul-tourist-information.com/en/public-transport-in-istanbul/

SABIHA GOKCEN AIRPORT TERMINAL SERVICES. (n.d.). SABIHA GOKCEN AIRPORT TERMINAL SERVICES. https://airport.online/sabiha-gokcen-airport-saw/en/sabiha-gokcen-airport-terminal-services

Tourism Information Offices. (n.d.). Istanbul.ktb.gov.tr. https://istanbul.ktb.gov.tr/EN-284752/tourism-information-offices.html

Deggin, C. (2023, October 10). The Istanbul European Side - The Most Important Part of Turkey. Property Turkey. https://www.propertyturkey.com/blog-turkey/the-istanbul-european-side-the-most-important-part-of-turkey

European side. (n.d.). Visit Istanbul. https://visitistanbulofficial.com/neighborhoods/european-side/

European Side of Istanbul. (2023, November 26). Turkey Visa Online. https://www.visa-turkey.org/european-side-of-istanbul

European Side Of Istanbul: Things To Do & See, Places To Visit, How To Get Around. (2023, March 28). ISTANBUL.TIPS. https://istanbul.tips/guide-about-european-side-of-istanbul-things-to-do-see-how-to-get-around/

Istanbul European Side Area Guide - Turkey Homes. (2020). Turkeyhomes.com. https://www.turkeyhomes.com/turkey-info/istanbul-european-area-guide

Voyage, E. F. (2022, March 23). Where to Stay in Istanbul, Turkey. ET Food Voyage. https://www.etfoodvoyage.com/where-to-stay-in-istanbul-turkey/

Asian side. (n.d.). Visit Istanbul. https://visitistanbulofficial.com/neighborhoods/asian-side/

Deggin, C. (2023, November 21). What to see on the Asian side of Istanbul. Property Turkey. https://www.propertyturkey.com/blog-turkey/what-to-see-on-the-asian-side-of-Istanbul

Istanbul Asian Side Area Guide - Turkey Homes. (n.d.). Www.turkeyhomes.com. https://www.turkeyhomes.com/turkey-info/istanbul-asian-area-guide

The Things To Do On The Asian Side Of Istanbul: Places, Districts, Cafe, And Top Attractions (2023). (2023, March 30). ISTANBUL.TIPS. https://istanbul.tips/discover-the-best-things-to-do-on-the-asian-side-of-istanbul-places-districts-and-top-attractions-2023/

Anya. (2021, March 4). Burgaz Island Near Istanbul - The Most Romantic Princes' Island. Road Is Calling. https://www.roadiscalling.com/burgaz-island-near-istanbul-the-most-romantic-princes-island-among-all/

Burgazada (Burgaz Island). (n.d.). Www.visitingistanbul.com. http://www.visitingistanbul.com/burgazada.html

Burgazada İstanbul GoTürkiye. (n.d.). Goistanbulturkiye.com. https://istanbul.goturkiye.com/burgazada

Burgazada Princes' Islands. (2019, February 21). https://istanbul-tourist-information.com/en/experience-istanbul/princes-islands-adalar/burgazada-princes-islands/

Büyükada. (n.d.). Atlas Obscura. https://www.atlasobscura.com/places/buyukada#:~:text=B%C3%BCy%C3%BCkada%2C%20or%20%E2%80%9Cbig%20island%2C

Erlend. (2010, March 29). Is Büyükada the Only Princes' Island of Istanbul I Should Visit? - Istanbul Insider -. Istanbul Insider. https://theistanbulinsider.com/is-buyukada-the-only-princes-island-of-istanbul-i-should-visit/

Heybeliada İstanbul GoTürkiye. (n.d.). Goistanbulturkiye.com. https://istanbul.goturkiye.com/heybeliada

Heybeliada Princes' Islands. (2019, February 21). https://istanbul-tourist-information.com/en/experience-istanbul/princes-islands-adalar/heybeliada-princes-islands/

Istanbul Princes Islands, Istanbul Princes Islands Information. (n.d.). Www.acetestravel.com. https://www.acetestravel.com/Istanbul-Princes-Islands

İstanbul-Buyukada Hotels. (n.d.). Small and Boutique Hotels Website. https://www.boutiquesmallhotels.com/what-to-buy-in-buyukada

Kinaliada | istanbul.com. (2022, September 27). Istanbul.com. https://istanbul.com/travel/kinaliada

Kınalıada İstanbul GoTürkiye. (n.d.). Goistanbulturkiye.com. https://istanbul.goturkiye.com/kinaliada

Kınalıada Princes' Islands. (2019, February 21). https://istanbul-tourist-information.com/en/experience-istanbul/princes-islands-adalar/kinaliada-princes-islands/

Places to Visit in Kınalıada | Turkish Airlines Blog. (2022, March 22). Turkish Airlines Blog. https://blog.turkishairlines.com/en/islands-of-istanbul-kinaliada/

Places to Visit on Heybeliada | Turkish Airlines Blog. (2022, March 22). Turkish Airlines Blog. https://blog.turkishairlines.com/en/islands-of-istanbul-heybeliada/

Princes Islands in Istanbul | All About Turkey. (n.d.). Www.allaboutturkey.com. https://www.allaboutturkey.com/istanbul_island.html

Soumya. (2023, April 6). 13 Best Things To Do In Buyukada Istanbul In 2024. Stories by Soumya. https://www.storiesbysoumya.com/buyukada-istanbul-things-to-do/

Teknevia. (2023, April 2). Kınalıada: Historical Background - Teknevia. https://www.teknevia.com/blog/en/kinaliada-historical-background/

What to see and do in the Princes' Islands. (n.d.). Barceló Experiences. https://www.barcelo.com/guia-turismo/en/turkey/estambul/things-to-do/princes-islands/

Why You Should Spend A Day in Buyukada. (2019, June 25). Istanbultouristpass.com. https://istanbultouristpass.com/here-is-why-you-should-spend-a-day-in-buyukada

Yokuz, B. E. (2019, October 21). COMPLETE GUIDE TO THE BUYUKADA ISLAND, ISTANBUL. Biz Evde Yokuz. https://www.bizevdeyokuz.com/en/buyukada-island/

Deggin, C. (2019, May 17). 13 Things to do in Uskudar: Exploring Istanbul Neighbourhoods. Property Turkey. https://www.propertyturkey.com/blog-turkey/13-things-to-do-in-uskudar-exploring-istanbul-neighbourhoods

Engül, S. (2022, January 29). Shopping Streets & Malls in Kadikoy (Updated 2024). Istanbul Clues. https://istanbulclues.com/shopping-places-kadikoy/

Hotels in Uskudar, Istanbul. (n.d.). Booking.com. https://www.booking.com/district/tr/istanbul/uskudar.html

Kadikoy and Uskudar - a Guide to Istanbul's Asian side. (2023, September 7). HairlineTransplantTurkey.com. https://hairlinetransplantturkey.com/tips/kadikoy-and-uskudar/

THE 10 BEST Things to Do in Uskudar (Updated 2024). (n.d.). Tripadvisor. https://www.tripadvisor.com/Attractions-g293974-Activities-zfn7811850-Istanbul.html

Erlend. (2013, February 18). Where to Stay in Istanbul - Beyoglu or Sultanahmet. Istanbul Insider. https://theistanbulinsider.com/where-to-stay-in-istanbul-beyoglu-or-sultanahmet/

Estate, I. R. (2021, January 12). Information about Beyoglu in Istanbul – Explore them in Detail. Imtilak Real Estate. https://www.imtilak.net/en/turkey/articles/beyoglu-district-in-istanbul

Nicky. (2023, July 1). How To Choose Between Sultanahmet Or Beyoglu. Chasing the Donkey. https://www.chasingthedonkey.com/where-is-better-to-stay-in-istanbul-sultanahmet-or-beyoglu/

THE 10 BEST Things to Do in Sisli (Updated 2024). (n.d.). Tripadvisor. https://www.tripadvisor.com/Attractions-g293974-Activities-zfn7811854-Istanbul.html

Kucheran, Kashlee. The Perfect 3-Day Istanbul Itinerary. Travel off Path, 16 Oct. 2022, www.traveloffpath.com/the-perfect-3-day-istanbul-itinerary/.

Letschert, Gordon. 3 Amazing Istanbul Itineraries: For 4, 7 & 10 Days. Ways of the World, 6 Feb. 2022, www.waysoftheworldblog.com/istanbul-itinerary/.

Lush, Emily. 4 Days in Istanbul: An Unconventional Istanbul Itinerary. Https://Wander-Lush.org/, 26 Nov. 2022, https://wander-lush.org/4-days-in-istanbul-itinerary/

Paul, and Mark. 5-Day Istanbul Itinerary + Map, Tips & Where to Stay. Anywhere We Roam, 12 Aug. 2022, anywhereweroam.com/5-day-istanbul-itinerary/.

Planet, Drifter. How to Spend 3 Days in Istanbul (Itinerary), Turkey + MAP - Drifter Planet. Drifter Planet, 25 Nov. 2023, drifterplanet.com/3-days-in-istanbul-itinerary/.

HOW TO GET FROM Istanbul to Bursa. (n.d.). HOW to GET from Istanbul to Bursa. https://www.rome2rio.com/s/Istanbul/BursaA. POWELL, E. (2015, February). Sunken Byzantine Basilica - Archaeology Magazine. Www.archae-ology.org. https://archaeology.org/issues/161-1501/features/2789-turkey-sub-merged-byzantine-basilica

Daily Sapanca and Masukiye Tour: Full-Day Trip From Istanbul | alldailytours.com. (2023, October 18). All Daily Tours. https://alldailytours.com/turkey-dai-ly-tours/daily-sapanca-and-masukiye-tour-full-day-trip-from-istanbul#:~:tex-t=Sapanca%20and%20Masukiye%20Day%20Tour%20is%20available%20every%20day%20from

Dulger, K. A. and E. (n.d.). Green Mosque – Bursa || Turkey Tour Organizer. Www.turkeytourorganizer.com. https://www.turkeytourorganizer.com/blog/green-mosque-bursa

Freelancer, W. (2019, November 20). Edirne Facts, Worksheets, Etymology & History For Kids. KidsKonnect. https://kidskonnect.com/places/edirne/#Key_Facts_Information

HOW TO GET FROM Istanbul to Edirne. (n.d.). HOW to GET from Istanbul to Edirne. https://www.rome2rio.com/s/Istanbul/Edirne

HOW TO GET FROM Istanbul to İznik. (n.d.). HOW to GET from Istanbul to İznik. https://www.rome2rio.com/s/Istanbul/%C4%B0znik

Iznik (Nicaea) | All About Turkey. (n.d.). Allaboutturkey.com. https://allabout-turkey.com/iznik.html

Iznik | istanbul.com. (2023, April 12). Istanbul.com. https://istanbul.com/trav-el/iznik

Karaboga, E. (2023, July 25). 8 Best Restaurants in Edirne Today - Turkey Things. 8 Best Restaurants in Edirne Today. https://turkeythings.com/best-restaurants-in-edirne/#1-asma-alti-ocakbasi-restaurant-savor-authen-tic-turkish-flavors

Kemp, L. (2023, December 22). The City of Bursa Turkey: A travel guide. Www.encounterstravel.com. https://www.encounterstravel.com/blog/bur-sa-turkey

Kırkpınar Oil Wrestling Festival. (n.d.). Kırkpınar Oil Wrestling Festival. https://goturkiye.com/blog/kirkpinar-oil-wrestling-festival

Masukiye, Sapanca, Turkey - Holidify. (n.d.). Www.holidify.com. https://www.holidify.com/places/sapanca/masukiye-sightseeing-1268335.html

Ormanya, Sapanca, Turkey - Holidify. (n.d.). Www.holidify.com. https://holidify.com/places/sapanca/ormanya-sightseeing-1268357.html

Sapanca Lake, Sapanca, Turkey - Holidify. (n.d.). Www.holidify.com. https://www.holidify.com/places/sapanca/sapanca-lake-sightseeing-1268280.html

Silk Bazaar. (n.d.). Bursa Turizm Portalı | GotoBursa. https://gotobursa.com.tr/en/mekan/silk-bazaar-118/

Tom. (2023, August 8). Princes' Islands - Guide For a Daytrip From Istanbul. HairlineTransplantTurkey.com. https://hairlinetransplantturkey.com/tips/a-day-trip-to-princes-islands/

Top Things To Do In Bursa. (n.d.). Evisa-To-Turkey.com. https://evisa-to-turkey.com/news/top-things-to-do-in-bursa/

Top Things To Do In Edirne. (n.d.). Evisa-To-Turkey.com. https://evisa-to-turkey.com/news/top-things-to-do-in-edirne/

tourzim, S. (2020, June 17). Detailed Information about Sapanca and Masukiye: Sapanca – Masukiye Trip. Safaraq Tourzim. https://www.safaraq.com/en/blog/information-about-sapanca-masukiye#automated-offer

Veldwijk, I. (2021, December 1). Selimiye Mosque, Edirne (Turkey)—Ottoman Wonder of the Turks • Mind of a Hitchhiker. Mind of a Hitchhiker. https://mindofahitchhiker.com/selimiye-mosque-edirne-turkey-ottoman-wonder/

Babbel.com, and Lesson Nine GmbH. 5 Tips to Learn Turkish (from a Turkish Linguist). Babbel Magazine, 13 Aug. 2018, www.babbel.com/en/magazine/tips-to-learn-turkish.

Richards, Olly. 51 Common Turkish Phrases – StoryLearning. StoryLearning, 1 Mar. 2021, storylearning.com/learn/turkish/turkish-tips/turkish-phrases/.

The Turkish Language - Essential Holiday Phrases. Www.theturquoisecollection.com, www.theturquoisecollection.com/turkish-language/.

Turkish Phrases - Top 10 Turkish Sentences You Should Know! Www.mondly.com, www.mondly.com/turkish-phrases-expressions.

Türkiye Bursları - Tips for Learning Turkish for International Students. Www.turkiyeburslari.gov.tr, www.turkiyeburslari.gov.tr/page/student-story3-5

IMAGE SOURCES

1 https://commons.wikimedia.org/wiki/File:Istanbul-map-blank.svg

2 See page for author, CC BY 3.0 <https://creativecommons.org/licenses/by/3.0>, via Wikimedia Commons: https://commons.wikimedia.org/wiki/File:Istanbul location_districts.svg

3 User: (WT-shared) Shoestring at wts wikivoyage, CC BY-SA 4.0 <https://creativecommons.org/licenses/by-sa/4.0>, via Wikimedia Commons: https://commons.wikimedia.org/wiki/File:A_cup_of_traditional_styled_tea,_Istanbul,_Turkey.JPG

4 No machine-readable author provided. Rainer Zenz assumed (based on copyright claims). CC BY-SA 3.0 <http://creativecommons.org/licenses/by-sa/3.0/>, via Wikimedia Commons: https://commons.wikimedia.org/wiki/File:Lahmacun.jpg

5 A.Savin, FAL, via Wikimedia Commons: https://commons.wikimedia.org/wiki/File:Istanbul_asv2021-11_img72_IST_Airport.jpg

6 https://commons.wikimedia.org/wiki/File:%D0%98%D0%B7%D1%82%D0%BE%D1%87%D0%BD%D0%B0_%D0%A2%D1%80%D0%B0%D0%BA%D0%B8%D1%8F_%D0%BD%D0%B0_%D0%BA%D0%B0%D1%80%D1%82%D0%B0%D1%82%D0%B0_%D0%BD%D0%B0_%D0%9C%D0%B0%D1%80%D0%BC%D0%B0%D1%80%D0%B0,_%D0%A2%D1%83%D1%80%D1%86%D0%B8%D1%8F.png

7 Arild Vågen, CC BY-SA 3.0 <https://creativecommons.org/licenses/by-sa/3.0>, via Wikimedia Commons: https://commons.wikimedia.org/wiki/File:Hagia_Sophia_Mars_2013.jpg

8 Constantin Barbu, CC BY 2.0 <https://creativecommons.org/licenses/by/2.0>, via Wikimedia Commons: https://commons.wikimedia.org/wiki/File:The_Blue_Mosque_at_sunset.jpg

9 Slyronit, CC BY-SA 4.0 <https://creativecommons.org/licenses/by-sa/4.0>, via Wikimedia Commons: https://commons.wikimedia.org/wiki/File:Topkapi_Palace.jpg

10 Moise Nicu, CC BY 3.0 <https://creativecommons.org/licenses/by/3.0>, via Wikimedia Commons: https://commons.wikimedia.org/wiki/File:Basilica_Cistern_Istanbul.JPG

11 Roger W from Sarasota, Florida, U.S.A., CC BY-SA 2.0 <https://creativecommons.org/licenses/by-sa/2.0>, via Wikimedia Commons: https://commons.wikimedia.org/wiki/File:Istanbul_-_Hippodrome_(3494147224).jpg

12 Laima Gūtmane (simka..., CC BY-SA 3.0 <https://creativecommons.org/licenses/by-sa/3.0>, via Wikimedia Commons: https://commons.wikimedia.org/wiki/File:Bozdo%C4%A3an_Kemeri_-_panoramio.jpg

13 MilenaBal, CC BY-SA 4.0 <https://creativecommons.org/licenses/by-sa/4.0>, via Wikimedia Commons: https://commons.wikimedia.org/wiki/File:S%C3%BCleymaniye_Mosque_01.jpg

14 Maksym Kozlenko, CC BY-SA 4.0 <https://creativecommons.org/licenses/by-sa/4.0>, via Wikimedia Commons: https://commons.wikimedia.org/wiki/File:2019-07-28_Galata_Bridge_1.jpg

15 Mark Ahsmann, CC BY-SA 4.0 <https://creativecommons.org/licenses/by-sa/4.0>, via Wikimedia Commons: https://commons.wikimedia.org/wiki/File:Istiklal_Avenue_in_Istanbul_-_Turkey.jpg

16 BLNTGRKS, CC BY 3.0 <https://creativecommons.org/licenses/by/3.0>, via Wikimedia Commons https://commons.wikimedia.org/wiki/File:Sakin_Bak%C4%B1rk%C3%B6y_-_panoramio.jpg

17 R Prazeres, CC BY-SA 4.0 <https://creativecommons.org/licenses/by-sa/4.0>, via Wikimedia Commons https://commons.wikimedia.org/wiki/File:Eyup_Sultan_Mosque_DSCF9637.jpg

18 Modris Putns, CC BY-SA 3.0 <https://creativecommons.org/licenses/by-sa/3.0>, via Wikimedia Commons: https://commons.wikimedia.org/wiki/File:Rumeli_Hisari_fortress_in_Istanbul_-_panoramio.jpg

19 https://commons.wikimedia.org/wiki/File:%D0%98%D0%B7%D1%82%D0%BE%D1%87%D0%BD%D0%B0_%D0%A2%D1%80%D0%B0%D0%BA%D0%B8%D1%8F_%D0%BD%D0%B0_%D0%BA%D0%B0%D1%80%D1%82%D0%B0%D1%82%D0%B0_%D0%BD%D0%B0_%D0%9C%D0%B0%D1%80%D0%BC%D0%B0%D1%80%D0%B0,_%D0%A2%D1%83%D1%80%D1%86%D0%B8%D1%8F.png

20 *flowcomm, CC BY 2.0 <https://creativecommons.org/licenses/by/2.0>, via Wikimedia Commons: https://commons.wikimedia.org/wiki/File:Anadolu_Hisar%C4%B1_in_2024_(cropped).jpg*

21 *RIFAT AĞAR, CC BY-SA 4.0 <https://creativecommons.org/licenses/by-sa/4.0>, via Wikimedia Commons: https://commons.wikimedia.org/wiki/File:Polenezk%C3%B6y_Tabiat_Park%C4%B1,_%C4%B0stanbul,_EOS_60D.jpg*

22 *LoudHmen, CC BY-SA 4.0 <https://creativecommons.org/licenses/by-sa/4.0>, via Wikimedia Commons: https://commons.wikimedia.org/wiki/File:Maltepe_mosque_3.jpg*

23 *Makalesta2, CC BY-SA 4.0 <https://creativecommons.org/licenses/by-sa/4.0>, via Wikimedia Commons: https://commons.wikimedia.org/wiki/File:Maltepe_Sahil_Park%C4%B1_Maltepe_%C4%B0stanbul.jpg*

24 *Roaa amer zatari, CC BY-SA 4.0 <https://creativecommons.org/licenses/by-sa/4.0>, via Wikimedia Commons: https://commons.wikimedia.org/wiki/File:Wotargarden_istanbol.jpg*

25 *Warmice01, CC BY-SA 3.0 <https://creativecommons.org/licenses/by-sa/3.0>, via Wikimedia Commons: https://commons.wikimedia.org/wiki/File:MuzeumhracekIstanbul_budova.JPG*

26 *User: Nastoshka, CC BY-SA 4.0 <https://creativecommons.org/licenses/by-sa/4.0>, via Wikimedia Commons: https://commons.wikimedia.org/wiki/File:Princes%27_Islands_travel_map.svg*

27 *Bulent Özden & Museum of the Princes' Islands, CC BY-SA 3.0 <https://creativecommons.org/licenses/by-sa/3.0>, via Wikimedia Commons https://commons.wikimedia.org/wiki/File:Adalar_muzesi_surekli_sergi_2.jpg*

28 *Jwslubbock, CC BY-SA 4.0 <https://creativecommons.org/licenses/by-sa/4.0>, via Wikimedia Commons: https://commons.wikimedia.org/wiki/File:B%C3%BCy%C3%BCkada_Rum_Yetimhanesi_(Old_Greek_Orphanage),_Istanbul_06.jpg*

29 *User: Darwinek, CC BY-SA 3.0 <https://creativecommons.org/licenses/by-sa/3.0>, via Wikimedia Commons: https://commons.wikimedia.org/wiki/File:Agios_Georgios_Greek_Orthodox_Church,_B%C3%BCy%C3%BCkada.jpg*

30 User: Darwinek, CC BY-SA 3.0 <https://creativecommons.org/licenses/by-sa/3.0>, via Wikimedia Commons: https://commons.wikimedia.org/wiki/File:Halki_seminary_(cropped).jpg

31 Oblomov, CC BY-SA 3.0 <http://creativecommons.org/licenses/by-sa/3.0/>, via Wikimedia Commons: https://commons.wikimedia.org/wiki/File:Heybeli_deniz_lisesi.JPG

32 Mesutsuat, CC BY-SA 4.0 <https://creativecommons.org/licenses/by-sa/4.0>, via Wikimedia Commons: https://commons.wikimedia.org/wiki/File:Heybeliada_Sanatoryumu.jpg

33 Bernd Hüttemann, CC BY-SA 3.0 <https://creativecommons.org/licenses/by-sa/3.0>, via Wikimedia Commons: https://commons.wikimedia.org/wiki/File:Synagoge_Heybeliada_2013.jpg

34 E4024, CC BY-SA 4.0 <https://creativecommons.org/licenses/by-sa/4.0>, via Wikimedia Commons: https://commons.wikimedia.org/wiki/File:Island_mosque_(K%C4%B1nal%C4%B1ada).jpg

35 https://commons.wikimedia.org/wiki/File:Istanbul-map-blank.svg

36 E4024, CC BY-SA 4.0 <https://creativecommons.org/licenses/by-sa/4.0>, via Wikimedia Commons: https://commons.wikimedia.org/wiki/File:Fish_and_seafood_of_Turkey_in_Istanbul.jpg

37 Kurmanbek, CC BY-SA 4.0 <https://creativecommons.org/licenses/by-sa/4.0>, via Wikimedia Commons: https://commons.wikimedia.org/wiki/File:Haydarpa%C5%9Fa_Pier_and_train_station_in_June_2023_(1).jpg

38 Habip Kocak, CC BY 3.0 <https://creativecommons.org/licenses/by/3.0>, via Wikimedia Commons: https://commons.wikimedia.org/wiki/File:Kiz_Kulesi_Maiden_Tower_In_Istanbul_(22930227).jpeg

39 Julia Sumangil, CC BY-SA 4.0 <https://creativecommons.org/licenses/by-sa/4.0>, via Wikimedia Commons: https://commons.wikimedia.org/wiki/File:%C3%87aml%C4%B1ca_Hill_panoramic_view_01.jpg

40 David Stanley, Attribution 2.0 Generic, CC BY 2.0 <https://creativecommons.org/licenses/by/2.0/> via Wikimedia Commons https://www.flickr.com/photos/davidstanleytravel/6526102263

41 https://www.pexels.com/photo/kiz-kulesi-in-istanbul-17376016/

42 Ymblanter, CC BY-SA 3.0 <https://creativecommons.org/licenses/by-sa/3.0>, via Wikimedia Commons https://commons.wikimedia.org/wiki/File:%C5%9Eemsi_Pasha_Mosque-madrasa.jpg

43 Another Believer, CC BY-SA 4.0 <https://creativecommons.org/licenses/by-sa/4.0>, via Wikimedia Commons https://commons.wikimedia.org/wiki/File:Istanbul,_Turkey_(November_2023)_-_246.jpg

44 https://commons.wikimedia.org/wiki/File:Istanbul-map-blank.svg

45 David Berkowitz from New York, NY, USA, CC BY 2.0 <https://creativecommons.org/licenses/by/2.0>, via Wikimedia Commons: https://commons.wikimedia.org/wiki/File:%C4%B0stiklal_Avenue_-_Istiklal_Street_-_%C4%B0stikl%C3%A2l_Caddesi_-_Istanbul,_Turkey_(10583503243).jpg

46 GrandEscogriffe, CC BY-SA 4.0 <https://creativecommons.org/licenses/by-sa/4.0>, via Wikimedia Commons: https://commons.wikimedia.org/wiki/File:Galata_tower_01_23.jpg

47 Pangaea W, CC BY-SA 4.0 <https://creativecommons.org/licenses/by-sa/4.0>, via Wikimedia Commons: https://commons.wikimedia.org/wiki/File:Pera_M%C3%BCzesi.jpg

48 Acediscovery, CC BY 4.0 <https://creativecommons.org/licenses/by/4.0>, via Wikimedia Commons: https://commons.wikimedia.org/wiki/File:Dolmabahce-Palace-Istanbul.jpg

49 Slyronit, CC BY-SA 4.0 <https://creativecommons.org/licenses/by-sa/4.0>, via Wikimedia Commons: https://commons.wikimedia.org/wiki/File:Grand_Bazaar,_Istanbul_6.jpg

50 PlanetKorriban, CC BY-SA 2.0 <https://creativecommons.org/licenses/by-sa/2.0>, via Wikimedia Commons: https://commons.wikimedia.org/wiki/File:2012_Fall_in_Istanbul_Chora_Church_(1).jpg

51 Dosseman, CC BY-SA 4.0 <https://creativecommons.org/licenses/by-sa/4.0>, via Wikimedia Commons: https://commons.wikimedia.org/wiki/File:Cevahir_mall_7416.jpg

52 Myaymaz, CC0, via Wikimedia Commons: https://commons.wikimedia.org/wiki/File:Ma%C3%A7ka_Park_(October_2009).jpg

53 https://commons.wikimedia.org/wiki/File:Ihlamur_Palace_Ceremonial_House.jpg

54 OpenStreetMap Contributors https://www.openstreetmap.org

55 OpenStreetMap Contributors https://www.openstreetmap.org

56 OpenStreetMap Contributors https://www.openstreetmap.org

57 OpenStreetMap Contributors https://www.openstreetmap.org

58 OpenStreetMap Contributors https://www.openstreetmap.org

59 OpenStreetMap Contributors https://www.openstreetmap.org

60 OpenStreetMap Contributors https://www.openstreetmap.org

61 OpenStreetMap Contributors https://www.openstreetmap.org

62 OpenStreetMap Contributors https://www.openstreetmap.org

63 OpenStreetMap Contributors https://www.openstreetmap.org

64 OpenStreetMap Contributors https://www.openstreetmap.org

65 OpenStreetMap Contributors https://www.openstreetmap.org

66 OpenStreetMap Contributors https://www.openstreetmap.org

67 OpenStreetMap Contributors https://www.openstreetmap.org

68 OpenStreetMap Contributors https://www.openstreetmap.org

69 OpenStreetMap Contributors https://www.openstreetmap.org

70 OpenStreetMap Contributors https://www.openstreetmap.org

71 OpenStreetMap Contributors https://www.openstreetmap.org

72 OpenStreetMap Contributors https://www.openstreetmap.org

73 OpenStreetMap Contributors https://www.openstreetmap.org

74 Wayne Noffsinger, CC BY 2.0 <https://creativecommons.org/licenses/by/2.0>,
 via Wikimedia Commons: https://commons.wikimedia.org/wiki/File:Selimiye_
 mosque_Edirne.jpg

75 Yahia.Mokhtar, CC BY-SA 4.0 <https://creativecommons.org/licenses/by-sa/4.0>, via Wikimedia Commons: https://commons.wikimedia.org/wiki/File:Bursa_Ye%C5%9Fil_Camii_-_Green_Mosque_(35).jpg

76 HALUK COMERTEL, CC BY 3.0 <https://creativecommons.org/licenses/by/3.0>, via Wikimedia Commons: https://commons.wikimedia.org/wiki/File:Bursa-kozahan-silk_bazaar_-_panoramio_-_HALUK_COMERTEL.jpg

77 Paul, CC BY-SA 2.0 <https://creativecommons.org/licenses/by-sa/2.0>, via Wikimedia Commons: https://commons.wikimedia.org/wiki/File:IMG_Hac%C4%B1_%C3%96zbek_Mosque.jpg

78 Ahmet Kagan Hancer, CC BY-SA 4.0 <https://creativecommons.org/licenses/by-sa/4.0>, via Wikimedia Commons: https://commons.wikimedia.org/wiki/File:Lake_Iznik_(Iznik_Golu).jpg

79 https://www.pexels.com/photo/pink-background-with-speech-bubble-1111369/

Printed in Great Britain
by Amazon